YOU'RE ONLY OLD ONCE

Catharine Brandt

Illustrated by Audrey Teeple

AUGSBURG PUBLISHING HOUSE
MINNEAPOLIS, MINNESOTA

YOU'RE ONLY OLD ONCE
Copyright © 1977 Augsburg Publishing House
Library of Congress Catalog Card No. 76-27085
International Standard Book No. 0-8066-1570-2

All rights reserved. No part of this book may be used or reproduced in any manner whatsoever without written permission except in the case of brief quotations embodied in critical articles and reviews. For information address Augsburg Publishing House, 426 South Fifth Street, Minneapolis, Minnesota 55415.

Scripture quotations unless otherwise noted are from the Revised Standard Version of the Bible, copyright 1946, 1952, and 1971 by the Division of Christian Education of the National Council of Churches. Quotations from the Living Bible (LB) copyright © 1971 by Tyndale House Publishers. Quotations from the New English Bible (NEB) copyright © 1961, 1970 by the Delegates of The Oxford University Press and the Syndics of the Cambridge University Press. Quotations from Today's English Version (TEV) copyright 1966 by American Bible Society.

Permission to include quotations from the following books has been granted by the publishers:

The Baptism and Fullness of the Holy Spirit by John R. W. Stott, © 1964 by Inter-Varsity Fellowship, London, and used by permission of InterVarsity Press, USA.

The Upper Room Disciplines 1974, from the week of meditations written by Mrs. Jo Kimmel (now Mrs. Clyde Chesnutt), published by The Upper Room, Nashville, Tennessee, © 1974.

The Measure of My Days by Scott-Maxwell, © 1968 by Florida Scott-Maxwell, reprinted by permission of Alfred A. Knopf, Inc.

Manufactured in the United States of America

CONTENTS

Introduction	7
Face the Facts	9
There's a Road Ahead	13
"I Never Sit in a Rocking Chair Unless I Get Paid"	16
Exercising More than Caution	19
Make Your Own Music	22
Second Career	25
Is Someone Calling?	29
Plenty of Time, Nothing to Do?	33
Self-Starter	36
Private-Eye Snooping	39
Take Care of Yourself	43
A Place in the Sun	46
Fear Is a Loud and Noisy Thing	49
The Gift God Withholds	53
Heart Specialist	56
Give Yourself a Present	59
New Neighbors	62
Living with the Younger Generation	66

Out of Touch with Reality	69
Rainbows	73
On Speaking Terms with God	76
Who Will Take Her Place?	79
Explaining the Hope Within	82
Still Time to Sing	86
Marching Orders	89
Stumbling Blocks or Stepping-Stones	92
God's Knocking Time	96
Don't Desert Me Now	99
Sojourners	102
Blessed Assurance	105
Cutting Out Clutter	108
Silver, Gold, and Cattle	112
Only One Vote	115
Take Pen in Hand	118
Footwashers	121
The Time of Your Life	124

*To my friends and fellow writers of
The Robin and
The Saturday Club.
You have listened to and encouraged me
and enriched my life.*

INTRODUCTION

All of us can recall famous men and women who kept on working, inventing, producing and serving far into their 80s and 90s.

Most of them had special talents or were geniuses or made headlines. I admire such famous and successful ones, but with few exceptions they are not mentioned in this book. I don't know them.

But I do know scores of ordinary men and women who when they reached old age seized the time as a gift from God.

They crossed the threshold with expectancy. They joyfully grasped the promise "as your days, so shall your strength be," and they have grown.

It's your old age. It's my old age. But it happens only once.

FACE THE FACTS

The evening paper carried the headline, "Elderly man struck by car. Severely injured." The account stated the elderly man was 61.

I felt as if I'd been struck down myself. I was 61 and not elderly. Not me! That young reporter needed to learn a thing or two about age.

Before writing a protest letter, I peeked at Webster. The dictionary defines *elderly* as being old, past middle age. Flipping pages I read that middle age is that period of life from about age 40 to 60. Oh!

After the initial shock, I faced the fact of being statistically old. I felt a little like the time our four-year-old grandson came to visit for a few days. He had yelled with delight at the prospect of a vacation at grandpa's. Days beforehand he packed his red plaid suitcase. At our house I helped him unpack.

"Grandma," he said in a small voice, "why am I here for?"

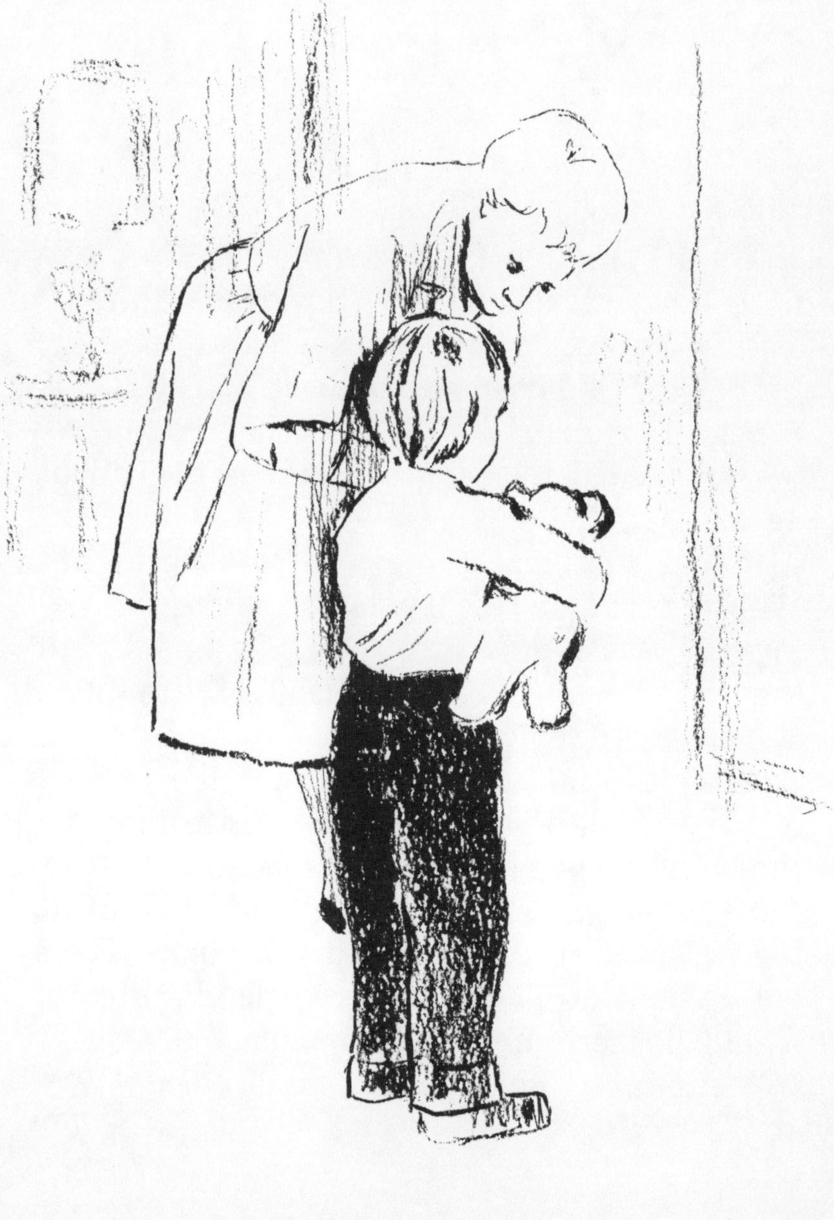

Recognizing the first sign of homesickness I drew him close. "Because you wanted to come, dear."

"No, I didn't. And when I was home I didn't miss you."

Not many ask for old age, nor have they missed it beforehand. And when we get there, we are bound to feel pangs of regret.

A friend in a large apartment-complex says, "For years I looked forward to retirement. Now that I'm 65 and retired, I find the future is not what it used to be. I get the feeling I'm out of it. They put me off at the wrong station."

Is old age only a time of feeling out of it, of homesickness for the past? Or are there bonus benefits?

Compensations do go with every period of life. Once I told a young friend, "I don't mind reaching middle age. Men still open doors for you and help take off your coat."

"But it's more fun when they whistle at you," she said with a giggle.

If whistles are a thing of the past, one of the compensations may be that, as a friend said, "Others ask for your opinion or advice."

"So old age makes giving advice legal," I said.

"Never," my friend replied. "Young people

may think I'm wise, but I'm wise enough to withhold advice."

What then are the compensations of old age?

As a young person I once declared, "I don't want to be old with wrinkles and crutches and with poor eyesight or deafness."

Now that I am old, I praise God for the gift of years, the joy of awaking to each new day, for muscles in action. I'm thankful for wrinkles (which don't hurt) instead of arthritis (which does).

Youth has energy and vitality. Middle age solves problems and carries responsibilities. Old age? That's the time to be ourselves, to fulfill objectives only dreamed about for years, to discover God's purpose for right now.

No one can snatch back the years and live them again. What we have is *today* and the priceless gift of life.

I will be your God through all your lifetime, yes, even when your hair is white with age.

Isa. 46:4 LB

O God, we can no longer fly like eagles or even run without being weary. But this is the only time we will be old. Show us what to do with these years.

THERE'S A ROAD AHEAD

"We should remove the word *retirement* from our vocabulary," declares Dr. James A. Perkins, an authority on the later years. Instead of talking about retirement, we should talk about changing gears, he says. The man is probably right.

The idea of retirement is a modern one. Whatever people in the Bible considered the business of life, they pursued it until they died.

Moses kept right on leading and advising, chiding and blessing the Children of Israel until his death. "Moses was 120 years old when he died, yet his eyesight was perfect and he was as strong as a young man" (Deut. 34:7 LB).

Still, mandatory retirement at around 65 is a fact of life in our country. We can call it changing gears, but we must face the reality of what retirement means.

In retiring we give up our identity as an employee, executive, or one who supplied a service. The problem is to find a new place of importance. Even though such activity may be intermittent, it should give meaning to life.

A retired corporation credit manager says, "I spent 16 years in school getting educated for a life in business, but very little time preparing for retirement. When the day came, they gave me a watch, and another man got my job. Like shutting the door in my face." Now he's looking for something to do that will help him know he's still on the turnpike.

For those already retired, it's not too late to rev up the motor and find a new road.

A former teacher now writes book reviews and is an authority on current books.

An over-70 minister volunteers for his church visitation program.

One retired couple distributes New Testaments to patients at the Veterans Administration Hospital in Minneapolis.

An over-80 organist is passing on her great skill to her pastor's daughter, teaching her without charge. "I don't need the money for my daily living," the woman says. "I'm glad to teach a young person my skills."

What knowledge or skill, obtained over a lifetime, do we have that we can pass on to others? Perhaps we don't understand new math or the Wankel engine or pro-football, subjects our grandchildren can expound on. But what accumulated experience or wisdom, perspective, or memories can we impart to others? What rich love or forgiveness have we experienced, what sorrow and tears that make us sympathetic to the needs of others?

Most of us when we reach 65 meet with fewer demands and less rigid schedules. When we change the tempo of life, there's time for detours, time to enjoy the world around us.

It is probably not true that life begins at 60 or 65. It is certainly not true that life ends there, or that it's time to idle the motor, or just park. There's a road ahead.

All of us must quickly carry out the tasks assigned to us by the one who sent me, for there is little time left before the night falls and all work comes to an end. John 9:4 LB

Lord, show us the road map for your God-conducted tour till the end of our journey.

"I NEVER SIT IN A ROCKING CHAIR UNLESS I GET PAID"

An 87-year-old friend of mine said that. She meant it too. No matter how long she lives, Alice Ruth Sherman will never be content to just sit and rock.

Part of her is an irrepressible sense of humor and a store of jokes and epigrams she pulls off the shelf at suitable moments.

"What some people call luck," she says, "may be the hand of God when he doesn't choose to sign his name."

Alice Ruth led a busy life earning a living. She taught diction and expressive reading to students from kindergarten through college age. For four years she broadcast a radio program of news for women. She wrote plays and poetry and lectured to groups. When her retirement date arrived, she breezed right through and began a new career. Now she is a professional grandmother model for TV, newspaper, and magazine advertising.

A recent ad shows her sitting in a rocking

chair, knitting, with an afghan spread over her knees. The picture represents the joy of old age when one has been prudent and built up a substantial account in a savings and loan bank. Nothing to do but sit back and rock.

Of course, a healthy bank account is desirable. But sitting in a rocking chair isn't Alice Ruth's idea of successful old age.

"Never!" she says. "Unless I get paid."

Even though we reach retirement age, all our capabilities are not turned off. None of us dare retire from responsibility, from living, from learning.

A 78-year-old widow with a small income lives with her granddaughter, her husband, and five children. The older woman remains active by supervising the children in cleaning up the kitchen after meals. She sews on buttons, mends rips, knits mittens, and tells stories to the children. Once a week she bakes bread.

"My granddaughter does the heavy work of keeping house," she explains. "Her husband works hard to provide for his family. I'm doing the little things they don't have time for."

Another woman, when she was 60 years old, faced a spiritual crisis in her life. A successful businesswoman and lecturer, she had turned her back on the church and God.

One day she listened to a minister present the claims of Christ. What he said rocked her out of her self-sufficiency, and she prayed to receive Christ as her Savior. Now she is going full speed ahead, telling others about God.

"Although I didn't know it at the time," she says, "my former work and life apart from God prepared me for my new life. Now that I'm retired I'm going 'like sixty,' learning all I can about the Bible because the time I have is short."

I take these older persons as my examples and have learned that we all need something to retire to. And never just a rocking chair. As one writer suggests, "We can withdraw from the front, but we should stay in the fight."

The happiest older people I know are determined to invest their abilities, depending on their strength, in productive work, service to others and the church.

They that wait upon the Lord shall renew their strength. Isa. 40:31 KJ

O God, when we are forced to retire from our jobs, show us you still have work for us. Give us courage to undertake the task, and strength and patience to perform it.

EXERCISING MORE THAN CAUTION

The other day in a restaurant I overheard two women, probably in their 70s. One said, looking grimly at the menu, "I'm not ready for lunch. I haven't had breakfast yet. I just got up."

"Why do you sleep so late?" the other asked.

"I tried getting up early, but it makes such a long day."

The second woman sat up a little straighter. "I have a date with life every morning. I can't wait to find out what God has for me next."

These two women demonstrate why various older persons differ in mental, physical, and spiritual health. People grow old when they begin to exercise caution about their hopes and dreams. Too much caution makes us forget the joy of living. Hardening of the attitudes often sets in before hardening of the arteries.

A few years ago at the annual meeting of the American Newspaper Publishers Association, the oldest editor present was 95. Of course he didn't look like a man of 35 or 40, but he talked like one and worked six full days a week.

Cor and Minka, in their 60s, departed from Holland to start a new life in the United States. Cor was an artist, and Minka had been a concert pianist.

Although the couple left behind them their lifetime customs and friends, they forgot caution and entered their new life with hope.

Friends in St. Paul, Minnesota, encouraged Cor to free-lance his superb paintings and etchings. Minka began teaching piano to gifted children and continued teaching well into her 80s.

All of us know plucky older men and women who, in spite of pain and strokes, radiate cheerfulness. They have a healthy mental attitude and a zest for living. These alert older people have several things in common. Besides taking reasonable physical care of their bodies, they also take care of their inner selves.

A frail, self-effacing woman in her 70s discovered the secret. She left her lifetime city home to be near her son's family in California. "I felt dependent, as if there was nothing for me to do, and I wanted to be cared for," she says.

She started going to a "senior citizens" group. At first she could scarcely climb the eight steps to the meeting hall. Soon she became interested in people, which led to her teaching a weekly Bible study at a nearby retirement center. Now she walks over a mile a day.

"God showed me life could still be interesting at my age," she says. "He literally renewed me physically, mentally, and spiritually."

We can't do much to check wrinkles, falling hair, the crick in the back, the ache in the knees, and the decreasing strength of advancing years—all of which are a great nuisance.

But the heart, the mind, the soul—there we have a choice. No need to wither and die inwardly. We can keep growing. When the inner self is nurtured and life is faced with expectancy, we forget about being overly cautious.

No wonder we do not lose heart!

Though our outward humanity is in decay, yet day by day we are inwardly renewed.

2 Cor. 4:16 NEB

Dear God, when we reach advancing years, don't let them be reclining years. Help us to limber up inwardly.

MAKE YOUR OWN MUSIC

One good aspect of old age is we can blow a horn, beat a drum, or play a harpsichord if we want to. We can even yodel.

All our lives others have tried to write the music for us. As young people, we found our peers and parents setting the tempo. As adults we listened to the boss, husband or wife, children and "what will they think," as they directed the rhythm, the volume of life's music.

But old age—ah, the melody can be our own. We can sound a few grace notes in everyday life or produce a hit tune if we're willing to risk a few discords.

Herodotus wrote that it is better to run the risk of a few anticipated evils than to remain a coward for fear of what might happen.

My own mother, in a day when wearing black was a symbol of lady-like maturity, blew a loud note when she announced she wanted a red dress. Red? That was for children and marching bands. Whoever heard of an old person wearing red then? She got the red dress. We loved her in it and were proud she dared to be different. Red suited her personality and her habit of whistling as she went about her work.

A young 68-year-old man I know works full-time. When the energy crisis hovered over us, he rode his bicycle to work three days a week, round trip 12 miles. He enjoyed the exercise and chuckled as one by one younger men where he worked started riding bicycles too.

"Aren't you afraid you'll get in the way of traffic? What if you have an accident?" some of us asked.

"Traffic better get out of my way!" he declared, as though he were beating a drum.

A woman in her 80s, who lives with a son and daughter-in-law, takes a month's vacation every year at a retirement center.

"That gives my son and his wife a vacation from me," she says. "They like their grandchildren to visit them, so I get out of my room and vacation at the retirement center." A world traveler in her younger days, the woman "explores" people in the home as she formerly explored other countries.

"When I return to my son's home, I have many experiences to relate, and so do they."

You're not sure what kind of music you want

to make with your life? Why not try a method young people use when they search for their talents? Draw a line down a sheet of paper. On the left side list 10 things you dislike doing. On the right-hand side list 10 things you would like to do. Things you've never dared try perhaps.

Take a long look at what you dislike doing. Can some be cut out, giving time to concentrate on what you like doing?

Counselors say that as we concentrate on things we like to do, we will find a way to do them. We will improvise.

Compose new songs of praise to him, accompanied skillfully on the harp; sing joyfully.

Ps. 33:3 LB

O Lord, when we settle down to doing things for the last time and never doing anything for the first time, teach us a new melody.

SECOND CAREER

A cartoon shows a man and his wife sitting in front of their mobile home. "You mean," the man complains, "that I spent 45 years knocking myself out for this?"

I don't know if that man did anything about his unhappy state, but one retired man and his wife did. "There has to be more to old age than nothing to do," he says. "My wife and I both looked for part-time work—something that would help our town, help other people. Then we heard about Foster Grandparents. We're having fun as grandpa and grandma to kids without even parents."

Authorities say that many in their 60s and older are capable of working and would be better off if they did. Older men and women push out into a second career for various reasons. Some, like the couple above, can't endure being inactive. Some need more money just to get by. Others want extra money to give to the church or to help people when disaster strikes.

Some find a second career with no thought of payment, just work that needs doing.

An aging person can test his idea of a second career.

- Is it a job that makes use of my abilities?
- Is it a job I can work at part-time for several years?
- Do I have the physical strength? Can I work at my own pace?
- Is it a job I like?
- Does it bring me in touch with people, where I can help others? Can I talk about my faith and what God means to me?

A successful engineer began studying for the ministry when he was 66. Now 84, he visits nursing homes and administers the Lord's Supper to shut-ins.

A woman started a second career with a school for the mentally retarded because her new grandchild was brain-damaged at birth. She wanted to help her son and daughter-in-law with their little one.

When Olga Soderberg retired from the school system, she set to work on a new career. She wanted to safeguard the history of Grand Marais, Minnesota. Her dream was to establish a historical museum on the spot where early fur traders landed after trekking across Lake

Superior from Canada. She fought local and federal red tape to obtain a building on the rocky shores of Lake Superior. Cook County Historical Museum now stands as a tribute to what one woman, working with interested citizens and historical society members, did with her retirement years.

Rural men and women may find the Green Thumb program a logical part-time second career. Sponsored by the Farmers Union, the Green Thumb is a federal project, now operating in more than 25 states. The program helps those on Social Security supplement their income through community and conservation projects.

Under the program older men build parks, transplant trees, resurface strip mines, repair and paint picnic tables. Both men and women provide reach-out services for shut-ins and the handicapped.

"After a few weeks in the open," one Green Thumber says, "I feel better, eat more, and sleep more."

Summing it up are the words of the grandmother of Edward Bok, who gave America the beautiful bird sanctuary and singing bell tower located in central Florida, "Make you the world a bit better or more beautiful because you have lived in it."

Lord, help me to realize how brief my time on earth will be. Ps. 39:4 LB

When our making-a-living days are over, Father, stir us up to find a second career, a making-a-life one, where we can help your people or care for your world.

IS SOMEONE CALLING?

Most of us while earning a living had little time for social and church volunteer work. Now these jobs may be piling up while we sit it out.

"It is not the possession of extraordinary gifts," says F. W. Robertson, "that makes extraordinary usefulness, but the dedication of what we have to the service of God."

Ask any of the following if they had extraordinary talents for their volunteer jobs. They would surely agree it was instead their willingness to give without getting that made them answer the call for volunteer help. And that in turn helped them retain their sense of usefulness.

"While I had an eight-to-four job, I couldn't do much volunteer work, which I greatly enjoy," says an active over-65-er. Now she gives her time one day a week to tape books and articles for the blind. She gets out the weekly news bulletin for her church. She heads the publicity committee for a national celebration and one for an educational group.

A retired school teacher, Phyllis McGee, paid her own fare to New Guinea, where as a short-term missionary, she taught the children of Wycliffe Bible translators. This freed parents for translation work.

When she arrived in Ukarumpa, black Christians crowded around her, touching her hair and kissing her. Phyllis admits she was startled until the missionaries explained the men and women were fascinated by her white hair and light skin.

Later she spent short terms in Brazil and Colombia. "I loved my work in South America," she says. "Some days I wanted to stay the rest of my life. But when lizards, ants, spiders, roaches, and chiggers moved into our room and on us, I wasn't so sure!"

A 90-year-old man was the oldest volunteer ever to work at St. John's Hospital, St. Paul, Minnesota. Twice a week, until his health failed last year, he spent five to seven hours feeding about 900 sterilized thermometers into a drying machine, then inserting them in sterile bags, ready for use again.

An 80-year-old housebound woman in California with talent for playing hymns puts a classified ad in the paper, offering to play any hymn requested. When the calls come she places the receiver near the piano and plays the hymn. Often the person calling needs someone to talk to and pours out his problem. "I lend a sympathetic ear," she says.

Stan Johnson was 75 when his wife died. He didn't want to sit home and feel depressed, so he turned to his minister for counsel.

"The pastor took me to a high-rise where he has a visiting program, and told me to knock on half a dozen doors and visit people. Next he took me to the prison rehabilitation center. Now I'm busy two or three days a week." He adds, "I can't express the joy I have doing something for others without pay."

The initials in *Action/RSVP* stand for Retired Senior Volunteer Program. The program sorts out the talents and skills of people 60 and over, putting them in touch with local service agencies needing part-time volunteers. People who can't leave their homes help by mending for hospitals or telephoning.

Nobody knows how many man hours volunteers provide in social and church work, or how many people are helped. But it is estimated that tens of millions of volunteers are serving others. Volunteers not only hear the call of others, they also hear the Lord Jesus who taught the principle of service to others.

Meister Eckhart put it this way: "In contemplation you serve only yourself. In good works you serve many people."

Like the Son of man; he did not come to be served, but to serve. Matt. 20:27-28 NEB

Lord of love and compassion, forgive us for laziness. When we want to embark on a flight from life, ground us so that we heed your call for service.

PLENTY OF TIME, NOTHING TO DO?

A wise man once said, "All people are hampered from doing what they want. Young people lack money, the middle-aged lack time, and the old lack energy."

True, older ones may not have the energy they once had, so they can't do some things they would like. But they may have more time than when schedules were full. In the last third of a long life, time often piles up, giving the feeling of nothing to do. There is, though, plenty to do if we take on the job of helping one another.

High-rises, mobile home parks, retirement and nursing homes, and churches are crowded with people who need sympathy, a smile, a listening ear, or hospitality.

A psychology professor at the University of Minnesota says one quality that contributes to a long, vital life is sharing our feelings honestly with others and giving pleasure to others.

Giving pleasure to others kept an 80-year-old woman at a church retirement-home busy. When I called for an interview, the operator said, "Please call back. Mrs. Dahlin has just left to take one of our older women to the doctor."

My purpose in visiting Mrs. Dahlin was to find out how she was adjusting to living in the church home, but I already had a clue.

Light-footed, gentle-voiced, with a warm smile, Mrs. Dahlin visited bedridden patients, pushed wheelchair residents to the chapel or activity room, and helped wherever she could.

"I still have good health, my sight, and hearing," she said. "A long life is meaningless without the Savior and the desire to serve him."

Ken and Shirley Zimmerman sold their house, bought a trailer, and headed for Kentucky, where they joined the staff of a children's home. It was a dream they had had for 10 years while they waited for Ken to reach 62 and take an early retirement.

Ken, as maintenance man, spent the first two weeks repairing a dryer, hot water heater, electrical outlets, and broken windows. Shirley mends and sews and does the addressing of the monthly mailings. Along with everything else, the Zimmermans give the children love.

One woman uses her spare time to clip poetry, jokes, and wise sayings from magazines and papers. She pastes them in 3x5 scrap books, which she gives to shut-ins.

A frail woman does the mending and patching for her minister's family of school-age boys.

I recall reading an article that suggested no one should complain of nothing to do until trying three remedies: invite three persons to your home at different times: offer to help three persons; talk about your Christian faith to three others.

"I used to think I would do great things for God," a woman whom I admire for her serenity says. "Now I let his Spirit do little things through me."

Nobody ever tells us to stop meeting the needs of others, to stop being kind. And kindness is love right out in the open.

I was eyes to the blind, and feet to the lame.
Job 29:15

Dear Lord, when we feel there is nothing to do, or we dread long days, help us to accept them as a gift from you, an opportunity to bring love and pleasure to someone lonely.

SELF-STARTER

Long ago the Greek dramatist Aeschylus said, "To learn what is new is to remain ever young." It's a self-starter statement. The quickest way to run down is to lose interest in one thing after another. Or to repress curiosity and stop learning new skills, trades, studies, or new ways of doing them.

Most of us in our 60s have already spent time figuring how to build adequate income for retirement years. It's a wise person who also takes stock of his mental and spiritual assets. Instead of sliding into a rut, why not plunge ahead into new ways of learning and growing?

The study of gerontology has turned up the fact that the mind may stay young and keen and clear even in the 90s. The brain, authorities say, is like a muscle; the more we use it the more it develops.

I belong to a professional writer's group. Some of its members have not written an article or story for a dozen years. Others keep on writing year after year. Their curiosity and interest in people and what is new in the world continue to sprout and blossom.

One whose curiosity has prodded her to learn about people is Mildred Comfort. She has written 49 books, several of them in the past decade. In her 70s and 80s she personally interviewed and wrote biographies of such prominent men as Herbert Hoover, Lowell Thomas, and William McKnight of 3M fame.

Many older persons today quit school when in their teens. Now, with time on their hands, curiosity, and the desire to learn, they find classes open to them. A number of colleges and universities offer tuition-free classes to those over 65.

Typical of the steady trek back to school by older men and women is Julia. "Instead of sitting in front of TV all day," she says, "I went back to school to learn more about planet Earth."

Just the other day papers carried an account of a 78-year-old woman who received a bachelor of arts degree in English and music.

"Learning a foreign language is hard work," a man in his 60s says. "But the young people in class are courteous and the instructors helpful."

In her 60s a woman took a defensive driving course provided by the state safety department. "I've been driving for many years without accident," she says. "But traffic is double what it used to be. I wanted to brush up on my skills. The course made me aware of some hazards I had grown careless about."

Old age is a fine time to begin intensive study of the Bible. An over-70 man reads the Bible through every year, besides following a study program. Others take correspondence courses from Bible schools.

Happy go-ahead older people are striking out for mental adventure. They keep wondering, questioning, and learning. Of course it's work. But the bonus is lifetime enjoyment and a new awareness of God's world and how much there is to learn.

I will praise thee for I am fearfully and wonderfully made; marvelous are thy works.

Ps. 139:14 KJ

Father, when we keep talking about how the world was 20 or 30 years ago, remind us that younger ones aren't interested. Stir us up to learn something new.

PRIVATE-EYE SNOOPING

Since childhood when my mother read to us to quiet us for sleep, I've loved books. We four children listened to *Oliver Twist, Arabian Nights, Little Women,* and others. We could usually count on a book with beautiful illustrations being under our Christmas tree.

Today I keep three or four going at a time—books to relax with, books to snoop in, books to make me think. "Not to contradict and confute, nor to believe and take for granted...," as Francis Bacon wrote, "but to weigh and consider."

Rereading books read years ago is like meeting old friends the second time. *Cry, the Beloved Country* by Alan Paton, *The Dean's Watch* by Elizabeth Goudge, *The Nine Tailors* by Dorothy Sayer, *The Chronicles of Narnia* by C. S. Lewis are a few.

Many of my favorite books inspire me to live the Christian life, be a better writer or driver, understand people.

And, of course, the Book of Books—the King James Version, but also modern translations to compare shades of meaning: Revised Standard, Good News for Modern Man, The New English Bible, The Living Bible paraphrase.

How good God is to provide us with many versions. Those who spend a lifetime reading and studying the Bible never tire of its riches.

Because of my interest in reading, I was delighted when my friend Deborah made a suggestion. "Would you like to spend an evening with me once or twice a week reading books to each other?"

Would I? For over three years now we have read aloud, except for times of illness or when one of us has been away.

We take turns reading while the other embroiders, quilts, turns up hems, or looks up new words in the dictionary. We weigh and consider and question as we go along. Our reading has led us to rabbits and Iberia, hobbits and current events. We have read a Revolutionary War novel, books about World War II, and biographies of famous men.

Our first book was *Only One Earth* by Barbara Ward and Rene Dubos, one that headed us toward serious thinking about ecology.

We listened to Paul Tournier's advice in

Learn to Grow Old. Clinton Rossiter's *American Presidency,* an older book, turned out to be informative at a time of attack on the Presidency. Rediscovering Tolstoy's slim book *What Men Live By* brought us delight.

At the same time, I've been reading with a church book club. A committee chooses and buys the books, handing them out at our monthly Sunday afternoon discussion.

About 14 of us read the book at home, and, with a different leader each time, we spend an hour or two discussing the book. We follow Mortimer Adler's suggestions in *How to Read a Book*. One rule is to determine what the author is trying to do before criticizing the book as a whole.

We have read John R. W. Stott's *Confess Your Sins*, Thomas a Kempis' *Imitation of Christ*, Raymond C. Ortlund's *Lord, Make My Life a Miracle*, and other religious books.

One man said, "I really like this book club. I've read seven books this winter that I'd never have taken time for otherwise."

A nationally known speaker, his wife, and teen-age boys read one of the classics last winter. Each had a copy and took parts as though in a play.

None of this is speed reading, but rather tracking down enjoyment and enlightenment. No older person with eyesight can say, "I'm alone," when books fill a shelf at home or the library.

The intelligent man is always open to new ideas. In fact he looks for them. Prov. 18:15 LB

Dear Lord, thank you for worthwhile books and for eyesight to read.

TAKE CARE
OF YOURSELF

They sat in the shade of the maple tree in the June sunshine, the old man in his 80s and his grandson.

"Gramp," the younger man said, "What do you expect to get out of old age?"

Without a moment's hesitation the old man replied, "Exactly that—out of old age!" Then he added wistfully, "I'd like to be your age again and meet deadlines and not feel sciaticky."

At first the man's reply may win our approval. We'd like to backtrack. But when seen in the perspective of a lifetime, old age is to help us pull away from deadlines and think about what's up ahead.

It's too late to look in the rearview mirror and live the past again. Instead, seminars on aging emphasize "improving the quality of old age."

"Start out with the idea of taking good care of yourself," one gerontologist says.

If we want to live old age to the hilt, we had better take care of the body God has given us. The older we grow, though, the more fragile we become. Bones break easily and heal slowly. Parts wear out. Income is often inadequate for expensive medical care.

Taking care includes not being overweight. It may not be so bad after all to live on a limited income and unable to afford rich food. Dr. Paul Dudley White once said that the only way a rich man can be healthy is to exercise and eat as if he were poor.

Equally damaging to a healthy body are concealed aggression, hate, resentment.

Kathy and her neighbor Sonja went to the same church. Kathy harbored resentful feelings toward Sonja, and they clashed from time to time. One day the minister set up a workshop on the theme "Love Your Neighbor." He told his congregation to invite to the workshop neighbors they had trouble getting along with.

Kathy hesitated to invite Sonja. She probably didn't know of Kathy's resentment. Why drag it into the open? Later when the phone rang, Sonja invited Kathy to be her guest at the workshop. "Maybe we can get things straightened out," she said.

Sonja had known all along about Kathy's resentment. Going to the sessions together helped them to a better relationship. In time they laughed about their former feelings.

As far as we know, God has given the gift of humor and laughter only to mankind. His book tells us that being cheerful keeps us healthy, and that it is slow death to be gloomy all the time (Prov. 17:22 TEV).

The Apostle Paul knew about the infirmities of the body. God told him to forget his, for God's strength was made perfect in weakness. Paul's recommendation is: Present your bodies to God. It's another way of saying, "Put yourself into God's hands each day." And that's the best care anyone can take of self.

Fix your thoughts on what is true and good and right. . . . Think about all you can praise God for and be glad about. Phil. 4:8 LB

Help me, Lord, to so live that no one will ever question your lordship of my body.

A PLACE IN THE SUN

Vic Lindahl, a successful businessman, had anticipated a carefree old age. Then ill health forced Vic to retire early. His pension, social security and reserves would all be less than he had figured. Such rapid changes in life often add up to discontent.

At first the Lindahls dreaded the adjustments they faced. Then they put their future into God's hands. "Lord, it's not the way I planned it," Vic said. "Now you be in charge."

With an arm around his wife, Vic told friends, "We're back where we started: a small house, no kids, no cash. We're on the threshold of a new lifestyle. We're depending on God for a lot we always took for granted, and we're having the time of our lives."

Psychologists tell us that several items contribute to inner happiness or contentment, among them financial security. But Christians have a security that far outshines money in the bank. We are told not to live for money but to be content with what we have, for the Lord is our helper (Heb. 13:5-6 NEB).

It's the ability to say *yes* to new situations that makes growing older an adventure, a discovery in contentment, a place in the sun.

In times of adjustment or change, it helps, I've found, to have someone we can talk to about what the Lord is doing in our lives— someone with whom we can pray, laugh, and even weep.

An 80-year-old man who left his lifetime job 15 years ago says, "At first I thought fishing in Canada in the summer, sitting in the Arizona sun in winter, with cruises in between was the ideal life.

"Then illness sets in, stiff joints, you lose your teeth, the doctor puts you on a diet, and you begin to feel sorry for yourself.

"I'm glad I've always liked people. Now I'm letting God open up areas I never had time for while working."

Contentment is within ourselves, a 17th century French writer once said, and if we do not have it, it's useless to look outside ourselves for it. Those who make adjustments easily, trusting God for the future, know this is true.

One January day a business friend visited a man recuperating from a heart attack. The friend offered advice. "You ought to get out of Minnesota's 10-below-zero weather and blizzards. Fly to Florida. Sit in the sun. Watch the ocean."

The heart patient laughed. "What for? Here I sit in the sun and watch the cars get stuck, and the weather's always 72 degrees where I am."

As one man puts it, "Contentment is not having what you want, but wanting what you have."

Godliness with contentment is great gain.

1 Tim. 6:6 KJ

Lord of all, banish our discontent. Help us not to spin the wheels of our minds on bygone blessings, but to accept today's bounty and look forward to the promise of tomorrow.

FEAR IS A LOUD AND NOISY THING

Years ago when we were first married, my husband scratched his finger rather deeply at work.

"My hand hurts," he said that night. "I'd better soak it in hot water."

He was restless all night, and in the morning felt severe pain. When I saw two long red streaks up his arm, fear gripped me. Blood poisoning!

After calling the doctor we set out for the hospital. I was too frightened to talk about my dread, but it thumped inside like a bass drum. At the hospital nurses took over with hot packs and cheerfulness, and I left for work.

Alone at home that evening I read a magazine story about a young man with gangrene in his leg. The doctor amputated the leg, but the man died. My imagination took over. How would I ever get through this one? Would *my* husband die? I was honey-combed with fear.

When I reached the hospital in the morning,

after a sleepless night, I found he had recovered enough to go home the next day. Then I praised God and asked forgiveness for lack of trust. How foolish to listen to noisy fear instead of trusting the Lord.

All of us experience times of anxiety. In fact, as Paul Tournier writes in *Learn to Grow Old*, anxiety is inescapable. In such times many of us are high-level worriers. We must do something, so we worry. But fear and worry can sometimes cause physical reactions.

I am reminded of the new father who went home after the birth of his child and suffered severe chest pains. The next day a doctor examined him. After tapping and listening the doctor said nothing was wrong.

"Then what was the pain?" the man asked.

The doctor grinned and said, "Labor pains."

One of Lyndon B. Johnson's favorite stories was about a 93-year-old woman who gave her recipe for a long life.

"When I walk," she said, "I walk slowly. When I sit, I sit easy. When I feel a worry coming on, I go to sleep."

We read in the book of Proverbs: "You can sleep without fear; you need not be afraid of disaster . . . for the Lord is with you; he protects you (Prov. 3:24 LB).

Friends told me of a couple who had retired. They depended on the rental money of a building they owned for part of their income. When a tornado blew the roof off the building and toppled the walls, everything was destroyed.

"What will you do?" others asked.

"We trusted God in our good days," the man replied. "Now we'll trust him in the day of trouble."

Don't worry about anything; instead, pray about everything; tell God your needs and don't forget to thank him for his answers.

Phil. 4:6 LB

Dear Lord, sometimes fear keeps us from hearing your voice. Instead of trembling under an electric blanket, we can reach for your promises.

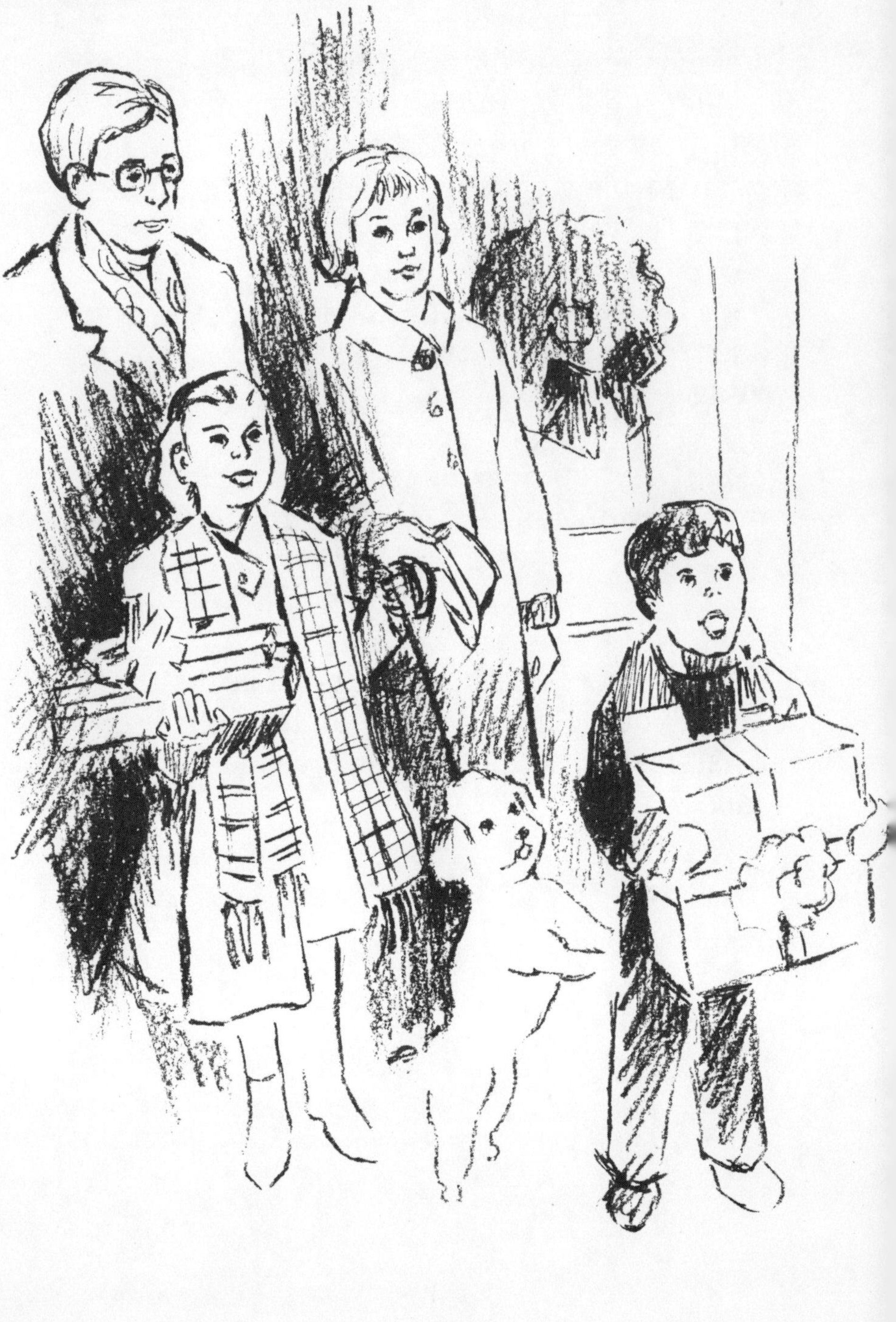

THE GIFT GOD WITHHOLDS

One Christmas my children and grandchildren visited me for a few days. They crowded my apartment with suitcases and long legs, hair dryers and superbowl games. We ran a relay race with shopping trips, big meals, and snacks. In spite of the work, I enjoyed every moment of their visit.

When the car drove away, though, I felt a blissful quietness, and I was as tired as if I had shoveled a driveway of snow. I set to work putting folding cots and dishes back in place. Then it hit me. Loneliness. I missed the warmth and love, the laughter and fun of young people, the joy of being with loved ones.

Most of us have had the experience of being lonely for absent parents, children, friends, husband, or wife.

A famous doctor explains the feeling. "We have a built-in desire to belong to someone who loves us. When they leave, we are lonely."

When I was younger, an elderly aunt said,

"One of the spiritual and mental pitfalls of old age is loneliness. The affliction can turn us into bores, make us self-centered or unhappy even in the midst of a crowd."

I recall thinking that loneliness would never get me down. My life was crowded with people and work and excitement. Sometimes I wanted to be alone. Of course, being alone is not the same as being lonely.

After talking to scores of elderly persons, I now realize that very few people under 60 have any idea what it's like to be old and lonely. Loss of loved ones, friends moving away, children leaving for lives of their own can cause us to be uncertain of the future, making us restless and lonely.

In the depths of our being is another loneliness, though we may not recognize it as such. It's a weariness, a yearning for God. It's a longing that can be present even when our need for human love is satisfied. It's a homesickness for God that can only be cured when we turn our lives over to Christ. In the words of Augustine, we are restless till we find our rest in him.

George Herbert in "The Pulley" tells us that when God first made man he poured on him multiple blessings. Then God withheld the blessing of *rest* to keep man from adoring his gifts instead of God.

Let man keep the gifts, the poem continues,

> But keep them with repining restlessness:
> Let him be rich and weary, that at least
> If goodness lead him not, yet weariness
> May toss him to my breast.

Human companionship alone cannot satisfy heart weariness. When we call to him, he answers that deep restlessness all of us have, and he puts joy in our hearts.

And ye shall find rest unto your souls.

Matt. 11:29 KJ

O God, disturb us when we want to hang onto loneliness for people and play the tape of self-pity. Draw us with your love and satisfy that greater loneliness we have to belong to you.

HEART SPECIALIST

"Ma" Jahnke was a heart specialist. Her own children called her Ma, but so did friends all over the city, across our country and in foreign lands. She kept a little room in her home ready for visiting ministers and missionaries.

Her own grandchildren loved her, but so did children from her church and neighborhood, and the inner-city kids she helped at camp.

For many years children trudged to her back door for a weekly Bible class, taught by another woman. After the youngsters shed their jackets and mittens, Ma Jahnke sewed on buttons, mended rips, and knitted new thumbs into mittens.

While the children listened to Bible stories and sang songs in the other room, Ma Jahnke hummed along in the kitchen. She gave each child a hug as he left and said, "Jesus loves you, and so do I."

She has been gone for some years, but the memory of Ma Jahnke's love for others remains in the hearts of those she touched.

Anyone can be a heart specialist. The essential requirement is love.

We don't need a shopping list to remind us of those who need love. They are all around us. The man whose wife died last week. Neighbors who have built an invisible wall around themselves, shutting others out. Teens in trouble. Children wailing for help.

A wistful woman in a wheelchair told me, "My husband has been dead for 20 years, and I've never been held close by another since. It's the touching that drives away loneliness."

I gripped her hand and held it, while inside my heart ached. Feeling sorry for others churns up our emotions. But feeling sorry is not enough unless it's followed by some concrete act of love. Some have never learned to express love. They wait for others to make the first move. But it's the love we give to others that counts. That's why sending flowers for a funeral or taking a kettle of soup to someone sick makes us feel better. We need to express love in other ways too.

If we love another, we want to make life as enjoyable for that one as it is for us. I once heard a middle-aged woman say, "God has dealt gently with me all my life. He has showered me with blessings and loving kindness. How can I be anything but gentle and kind to his children? When I see someone in trouble, I want to help that person find joy in the Christian life."

"I'm a hugger," a young woman says. And love flows from hugger to hugged and back again. A hug, a caress, arms linked, a hand squeezed are marks of a heart specialist.

I've noticed that when I'm exhausted, it's difficult to be kind and loving to others and to think of their needs. Fatigue drives me into a state of impatience and grumpiness.

Before we can qualify as a heart specialist we may need surgery on our own hyper-activity. We may need to get more rest, spend more time with God, leave room for his interruptions. Then we can make haste to be kind, and be quick to express love.

And may the Lord make your love grow and overflow to each other and everyone else.

1 Thess. 3:12 LB

Dear Lord, you have nourished us with your love. Forgive us when we hoard that love instead of giving love to one another as you have commanded.

GIVE YOURSELF
A PRESENT

Someone has said that if we count more than five friends we are counting acquaintances. I suppose counting *friends* depends on what we mean by the word. We want a friend who sticks closer than a brother, one who feels for us in our trouble and is ready to help, one we enjoy being with.

But shouldn't we also give to a friend that which we expect? Isn't friendship two-way?

"A friend is a present you give yourself." Finding those words of Robert Louis Stevenson's not long ago brought into focus for me the idea of counting friends. If a friend is a present we give ourselves, do we have to limit ours to five?

The daughter of a woman who is 75 said to her mother, "I don't know anyone who has as many friends as you."

Her mother replied, "My friends are dear to me, and I work at keeping them. I don't let one get away unless God takes that friend."

Anyone 75 years old probably has had scores of friends along the way. But friends do change. They move across the country and easily become friends in spirit, not fact. God removes others in death, or gives us new ones.

"For that reason," an acquaintance told me, "I try to make one new friend every year, just to replace those I lose. If I don't, I count that year wasted."

To my regret I remember friends who are no longer close because of my carelessness or theirs. Even distant friends can be cherished if we heed Samuel Johnson's advice. "A man, sir, should keep his friendships in constant repair." With the help of letters, the phone, the airplane, there's little reason for losing friends.

Once when I visited my brother and sister-in-law in California, they planned a dinner party. A great deal of adult conversation went on around the table, chiefly about books and writing. I noticed the only child present, the 12-year-old daughter of one couple, had a look of being left out.

Afterwards my brother set up a game table and the girl sat down with Scrabble. I followed her and said, "Let's play." Between turns we talked, and she told me about her school friends.

The next day the girl's father called my brother. "My daughter says that when she grows up, if she ever writes a book, she'll dedicate it to your sister."

I consider that one of the most endearing compliments I have ever received, the result of being friendly, a present I gave myself.

One fact of life older people learn is that no one can live for himself and be happy. The one who shows love and friendliness to others will have friends.

Counting friends? Count those who love us, those we love.

A friend loveth at all times.   Prov. 17:17 KJ

O Lord, it's nearly the end of the day, and we haven't made as many friends as we would like. Help us be alert for new friends, those you want us to befriend.

NEW NEIGHBORS

After selling all her belongings except what would fit into one small room, Selma moved into a retirement center. Besides parting with her home of many years, she said good-bye to old neighbors, her garden and the routines of life. Many changes all at once made her feel threatened—that she was on a dead-end street.

"Moving into a retirement center can be bleak until we look at the options," another woman said. "My son wanted me to live with his family. Let me tell you, that house is bursting with kids and dogs. They go in for stereo and noise." She shook her head. "I like peace and quiet, so I chose this home for the aged."

Living in a retirement home can be an adventure when one begins to put down roots. Listen to this woman. "At the age of 69 I moved into a home for the aged. After 10 years I still thank God every day that I live here. It's home," she says. "I have care and comfort and peace of mind." Of course, her feeling of home and peace of mind didn't just happen. Cheerfully, from the day she moved in, she worked at being a good neighbor.

In a retirement home you may not be able to pick vegetables from your own garden to take to the one next door. You can't stir up a batch of cinnamon rolls for coffee with a friend. But the nourishment of kind words, the sweetness of fellowship, means a lot to new neighbors.

When an elderly man and his wife moved into a retirement home, he spent half the time pacing the halls and watching the clock. "I don't want to listen to their complaints and twice-told tales," he said, referring to his new neighbors. Remembering that he had enjoyed teaching the Bible in his church, his wife suggested he start a Bible study in the home.

"With all those old women?" he asked. (He was 83.) But he got permission from the superintendent. The first Bible study was such a success his attitude changed, and he started two more.

In another retirement center a woman took her Bible and two friends with poor vision to the room of a bedridden resident. Each day she read the Bible for half an hour. The shut-in, as well as the brought-ins, enjoyed the visits.

Try settling down close to a neighbor and

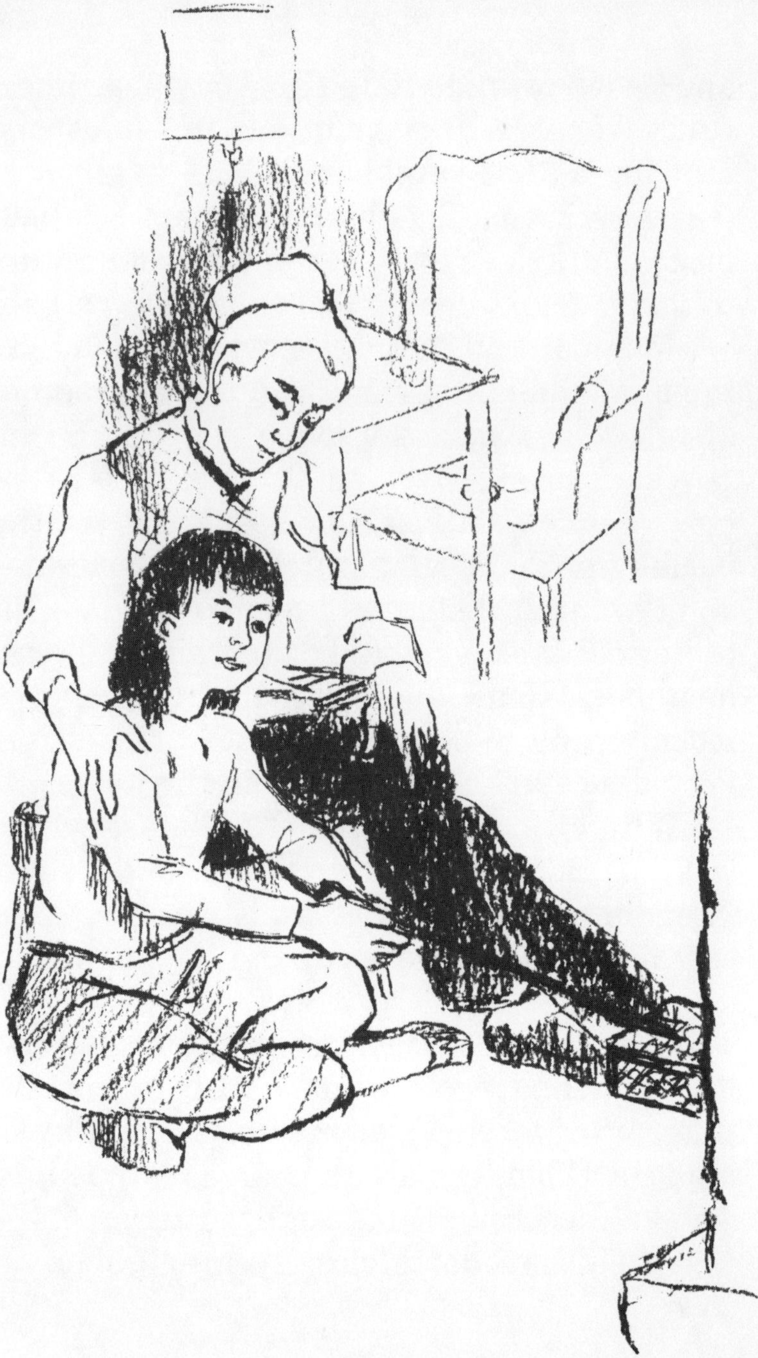

asking some of the questions ascribed to the Quaker faith: Where did you live when you were a child? How did they heat your home? What was the center of warmth in your house?

I have had a variety of answers to that last question. The kitchen stove. A one-register furnace in the living room. The dining room table. Dad's chair. Mother.

People love to talk about the past, and before we know it, we may uncover a need for which our faith has the answer.

It is also important to live in the present. As we take time to find out what new neighbors are like, we can give them a generous glimpse of ourselves, our hopes and fears. We can share books, magazines, treats, and above all our belief in the Savior.

If you and your neighbor have a difference of opinion, settle it between yourselves and do not reveal any secrets. Prov. 25:9 TEV

Heavenly Father, it's not easy to love and understand some of our generation, especially in close quarters. Others may also have trouble loving and understanding us. May your joy and love shine through us to our neighbors.

LIVING WITH
THE YOUNGER GENERATION

Clouds hung low in the sky and the wind swept across the bay, battering trees on shore. The young birches swished and arched with the onslaught. But the old scrub oaks and ironwood trees littered the ground with branches.

Snug in the little cabin in northern Minnesota, my grandchild and I read stories, played games, popped corn, worked with our hands. The cabin was heated by an airtight stove, big enough to hold logs and consume bushel baskets of kindling and twigs. Late in the afternoon the wind died down, and a moving cloud uncovered the sun.

"Let's fill the wood baskets," I told the child. Outside we stooped to pick up the branches, breaking them into suitable size. Of course the fleet-footed child filled a basket first.

"Grandma, do you always pick up wood for the stove?" I nodded. "You're pretty old to be picking up wood every day," she said smugly.

I laughed and said, "It's good exercise."

Grandchildren are often matter-of-fact about the age difference between generations. Grandparents, and parents, too, are old no matter where we are statistically.

But there's more than the age gap. Young people can't imagine growing up without blow combs and eye shadow, without pizza and snowmobiles. We older ones cringe at the decibels, disorder, and packed schedules.

Deep inside we know it takes longer for us to do simple tasks. Instead of hurrying and doing three things at once, we plod along. Serenity descends on us.

We welcome short visits with the whole clan, either here or there. It's something else when, because of ill health or other reasons, an older person moves in with a son or daughter. The feeling swoops down that giving up home means losing independence and position in life.

This need not be if grandparents stand on their convictions and pass them on to younger ones. One big advantage of a three-generation household is that young people learn to live with someone who may have different standards and ideas than they or their parents. At the same time grandparents who are most successful living with the younger generation are those willing to learn from them.

A friend who moved in with her son tells me that the biggest thing she learned was to keep quiet about herself.

"It's easy to forget that young parents may be irked by the arrangement, or at a loss how to make things work," she says. Instead of talking about herself, she tries to give warm and sympathetic words to others in the household.

Another widow, who lives with a daughter, advises, "Don't ever give the impression you feel neglected. And never criticize."

As we grow older, we often cherish ourselves and forget how very dear our family is and how much we both have to give.

The birch trees took the brunt of the storm at the lake, recovering quickly. But the old ironwood and scrub oaks parted with branches. When the twigs and branches were picked up and used, others were warmed.

We were ready to share with you not only the gospel of God but also our own selves, because you had become very dear to us.
1 Thess. 2:8

Dear Lord, give us wisdom and tenderness toward our own children, we pray, and make us easy to live with.

OUT OF TOUCH WITH REALITY

When I read of very old men and women being taken in by swindlers and losing their lifetime savings, I feel pity for them.

It's easy to understand their wanting to add to their small savings by a get-rich-quick scheme. I don't blame them for trying to get a new roof or furnace for the cheapest price, or to be cured of a disabling disease.

The truth is, though, some salesmen use unscrupulous frauds and swindles to trap the unsuspecting older person.

The U.S. Commissioner of Aging declares older persons are often taken in by frauds and quacks because they desire to talk to someone and receive mail, or they hope for a cure for pain or disease.

Wide-awake older ones are aware of such schemes and shut the door smartly or check out the deal with the local Better Business Bureau.

But not all older men and women are alert. Absentmindedness, disabling handicaps, or senility make some like children in their approach to choices and living. They are confused and easily taken in. When the confusion and disability get bad enough, relatives may arrange for them to go to a nursing home.

Such a person combats many losses. Hearing, sight, and taste. Loss of loved ones and friends, the familiar. Loss of financial security, perhaps. Loss of memory. Aches and pains. Open hostility or withdrawal may be the evidence of struggle and resentment against physical problems.

"I can't bear to visit Aunty in the nursing home," a middle-aged woman said. "She's nothing but skin and bones and sits staring into space."

According to Elizabeth Kubler-Ross in *Death and Dying*, even a senile person is entitled to dignity and tender loving care.

From time to time, before her death, I used to visit a dear friend in a nursing home. She had grown senile and did not remember me. I sat with her, held her hand, read a psalm and carried on a one-sided conversation with long pauses. When I rose to go she always said, "Don't go yet."

"How do you communicate with the senile?" I asked the chaplain of a nursing home.

"By love and touch and care," he replied. You can visit 10 times with no response, but one time, by the look in the eyes, outstretched hand, or even a few words, you know you have gotten through.

God gave me a beautiful object lesson when I helped with a nursing-home Bible study not long ago. It made me shed my coldness and indifference for those who suffer severe handicaps of old age.

Fifteen men and women, most in wheelchairs, sat around the table. A young seminarian, who called them "you guys" as a group, and by their first names individually, was in charge.

Their poor hearing caused the young man to shout, while helpers found the page for those who were almost blind. A former minister in a wheelchair, with a still powerful voice, pitched the hymns. They sang lustily and read the Scripture from large-print Bibles.

During the study the leader asked questions, which bounced back like a ball against a closed door. But once Emma answered. Strapped in her wheelchair, her hands and head shook violently with palsy. Somehow she got the answer out.

"Paul went back to Tarsus because Tarsus

was his home town, and he wanted his friends to know what happened to him on the road to Damascus." Who could say it any better?

Afterwards I said to Emma, "You've had a good life, haven't you?"

"A good life," she said with a smile. "God is good." The next time I visited, she didn't know me.

Cast me not off in the time of old age: forsake me not when my strength faileth.

Ps. 71:9 KJ

O God, how comforting it is to know that even though the mind forgets reality, you will not forget your own.

RAINBOWS

After picking up relatives at the airport, I drove them to their motel. On the way we encountered a heavy windstorm and a cloudburst. The storm lasted only a few minutes. Then the sun blazed through the western skies, and in the east a brilliant rainbow arched high across the murky clouds, both ends resting on earth.

The rainbow! Promise of God!

After the flood God made a promise to Noah. From then on the rainbow in the cloud would be a sign that God would never again destroy all living creatures by flood.

The Bible abounds with God's promises—rainbows. Most of us probably know dozens of Scripture promises. We memorized them as children or have read them as adults. We can scarcely believe the results of a recent Paris survey. Only one person in seven could name one of the four Gospels, and only one in 24 had ever opened a Bible.

Yet the Bible in various translations and paraphrases is the world's bestselling book. In America, at least, many of us own more than one copy.

At this period of life we have time to discover anew the power of God's Book to guide us and comfort us. Now is an ideal time to review familiar promises, to dig up colorful new ones, waiting to be tested.

Parts of the Bible are difficult to understand. But that shouldn't disturb us. Even great scholars are not in total agreement on the meaning of some Scripture passages. But God's promises are clear to anyone who will hear and do.

As British author John R. W. Stott says, "What is *described* in Scripture as having happened to others is not necessarily intended for us. Whereas what is *promised* to us we are to appropriate, and what is *commanded* we are to obey."

Not long ago I heard a man tell a group, "When life gets down to basics, we don't really care about some of those unanswered questions of the Bible."

We want help right now, help for our pain, our suffering, our fears. It cheers us to read God's promises that he will be with us, strengthen us, keep us from temptation, answer our prayers.

When life appears unbearable, we don't care to know what Paul's "thorn in the flesh" was. What strikes home is the Lord's promise, "My grace is sufficient for you, for my power is made perfect in weakness" (2 Cor. 12:9).

When we fear what will happen tomorrow, we're not much interested in eschatology (final events of the world). But what David says grips us: "I sought the Lord, and he heard me, and delivered me from all my fears" (Ps. 34:4 KJ).

Lord, why did this happen to me? "The hand of our God is upon all them for good that seek him" (Ezra 8:22 KJ).

Like a rainbow the promises of God arch above us and our lives.

He shall come down like rain upon the mown grass: as showers that water the earth.

Ps. 72:6 KJ

Father in heaven, you have given us great and precious promises in the Bible. May we search for them, believe them, and trust you.

ON SPEAKING TERMS WITH GOD

Two little girls visited their grandmother for a few days. At home before meals they prayed in unison, "Come, Lord Jesus, be our Guest," a beautiful prayer. But grandma chose her own words when she prayed.

One child said, "Grandma says so many different prayers."

The older child replied, "She makes them up in her head."

"Oh! She couldn't." The youngest child was skeptical. She hadn't begun talking to God.

Memorized prayers or those written by devout men and women often teach us to express ideas of the soul. But memorized prayers are not always speaking to God. How often have we repeated the Lord's Prayer without thinking about the ideas it contains? Hallowed be thy name. Deliver us. Thy will be done.

When we trust Jesus Christ to save us from eternal death, that is not all. We need a daily checkup so our lives are spiritually healthy.

"I do pray every day," a young woman once told me, "but I struggle to keep my thoughts on God." Most of us have had that experience. I know I have. Asking God to control our thoughts while we pray helps us think of his might and power, his love and mercy, so we can choose appropriate words.

Often our praying is spontaneous. Again, prayer is a battle because it takes thinking and determination and submission. And Satan doesn't want us to pray. He tries to make us forget to talk to God, or when we do pray to think about other things. Lunch with a friend. What to wear? Will it rain? There we are, turning our back on God.

Sometimes a different posture keeps thoughts on what we are praying. Try kneeling or standing instead of sitting. Pray with eyes open, looking out the window at something God created—marigolds or a bluejay or a tree laden with red apples.

Praying softly aloud, or at least forming the words with the lips, helps control thoughts.

Keeping a prayer list or notebook disciplines our thoughts. Perhaps we can't pray regularly for every relative and person we know. We can, though, ask God to bring to our minds those he wants us to pray for.

If we take time to consider their needs and talk to God about them, he may intervene in their behalf, or show us how we can help.

It's not true that people always draw closer to God as they grow older. Sometimes carelessness sets in. We may have to pray that God will give us a hunger for prayer as the poet Ralph Seager suggests:

Lord, lay the taste of prayer upon my
    tongue,
And let my lips speak banquets unto Thee;
Then may this richest feast, when once
    begun,
Keep me in hunger through eternity.

In talking to God no one has to deliver a speech, just a report of the day's activities—sorrow for sin, the desires of the heart, our hopes and fears. When we talk to God regularly, then wait in quietness, we are almost sure to feel his presence and his blessing.

I will therefore that men pray everywhere.
                              1 Tim. 2:8 KJ

We would be on speaking terms with you, God.

WHO WILL TAKE HER PLACE?

The average person who lives to be 70 years old spends:
- 23 years sleeping
- 19 years working
- 9 years playing
- 6 years eating
- 6 years traveling
- 2 years dressing
- 4 years unaccounted for
- 1 year in church.

How many years praying?

During the busy years of caring for a family, I often felt guilty because I found so little time for private prayer. Instead, after a quick reading of a few verses from God's Book, I hurled myself into the day's activities and prayed on the run.

Most of my on-the-run prayers turned out to be cries for help or a brief thank-you as I scurried from morning till night. Still I wondered why peace evaded me. Wasn't I following

Paul's advice — continuing instant in prayer?

One day God's Spirit showed me that I was crowding out God. I was begging for help, not taking time to know the Giver of help.

Long ago the psalmist wrote, "Be still, and know that I am God" (Ps. 46:10). The prophet Isaiah proclaimed, "In quietness and in confidence shall be your strength" (Isa. 30:15). Christ invited his disciples to come with him to a lonely place and rest a while. When we pray with the poet John Greenleaf Whittier, "Take from our souls the strain and stress/And let our ordered lives confess/The beauty of thy peace," God answers us.

But there's another result of quiet prayer—the power of intercession. One who understood the power of praying for others was a woman who lived in a nursing home. When she died at 87 years, her relatives provided a simple funeral. One, a missionary home on furlough, said, "I wonder who will take her place?"

Her place? She had lived her last decade quietly in the nursing home, but her sphere of influence encompassed the world. She had been a faithful intercessor for hundreds of missionaries. Knowing the power of her prayers, missionaries sent her their monthly newsletters and prayer requests. Every morning for two hours she wept and pled with God for the needs and trials of each missionary and his family. She praised God for answers and blessings.

After the woman's death letters poured in from missionaries around the world, telling how they had felt the support of her prayers. Doubtless she accomplished more through intercession than she had in her active years.

Who will take her place?

The earnest prayer of a righteous man has great power and wonderful results.
James 5:16 LB

Dear God, speak to us in our quiet moments. Please use us as intercessors for others. Amen.

EXPLAINING THE HOPE WITHIN

A mother with two young children waited in a doctor's reception room. Her little boy picked up a Bible story book from the table and climbed on his mother's lap.

"Read me," he demanded.

The mother began to read the story of Jesus asleep in a boat with the disciples when a great storm lashed them. The disciples panicked and wakened Jesus. "Don't you care that we drown?"

All at once the mother felt the quiet in the reception room. She looked up to find everyone listening to her.

"I didn't mean to read so loud," she said.

"Go on," one woman said. "I want to hear how the story comes out."

The mother read, "Jesus said, 'Peace. Be still.' And the wind stopped and there was a great calm."

"Did Jesus really stop the wind?" the child asked.

"Yes," his mother said. The low-key witnessing caught the other patients' attention and set them thinking before they returned to their own reading.

Reading my Bible the other day, I was again impressed by how Jesus took a group of unlettered men from the hills of Galilee and taught them the Good News. After his death and resurrection and before he disappeared from the disciples' sight, Jesus told them they were to be witnesses for him, by the power of the Holy Spirit.

The disciples took Christ at his word. They hiked up and down the dusty roads, and, empowered by the Holy Spirit, headlined the Lord's death and resurrection.

I used to think it took Bible school or seminary training to know how to witness, and that the task belonged to missionaries and ministers and evangelists. Then one day I read that Evangelist D. L. Moody said that he could not *make* men believe. That was the work of the Spirit of God. He believed God had appointed him to proclaim the gospel, and that's what he did until his death.

A young electrical engineer whistled at work. One day a new man started working with him. At lunch hour the new man asked, "Are you a Christian?"

"Sure am," the engineer said. "How did you know when we haven't even talked?"

"You're always whistling hymns."

The engineer hadn't been aware of his whistling witness, but it brought two Christians together.

Perhaps a clearer word than witnessing would be *explaining*. Simply explain to another person what Jesus Christ has done for you as Savior and Lord, what he is doing today, and leave the results to God.

A man scheduled for surgery one morning prayed that God would send him a room partner he could explain his faith to. When the man was wheeled back to his room, he found the other bed occupied by a patient of another faith. He made friends with the man and talked about what Christ had done for him.

We're not all ministers and evangelists, but we can know what we believe and explain our faith to others.

Be ready at all times to answer anyone who asks you to explain the hope you have in you.

1 Peter 3:15 TEV

Father, you have forgiven us much. Your Word tells us that by believing in the death and resurrection of your Son Jesus Christ we have eternal life. Give us courage to explain this to others.

STILL TIME TO SING

"Why doesn't the Lord take me home?" an 86-year-old woman asked her minister.

"Perhaps he wants to hear you sing a bit," he replied gently.

"Sing? I can't sing. Besides, when you're crippled with arthritis, and you have to be waited on, and you're running out of money, what's there to sing about?"

"Has God ever let you down?" the minister asked. "Perhaps all he wants is for you to be a hymn of praise."

As she listened, the woman gradually gave up her resentment. Later her attitude was replaced by a song in her heart. Some days, of course, she had too much pain to sing or act joyful. But other days she let the joy out, praising God to everyone who came into her room.

"I even sing out loud," she said, "when no one's around to hear my quavery voice."

As I recall the time tragedy struck our home when I was a child, the picture that comes to my mind is that of my mother singing with tears, "What a friend we have in Jesus." The sorrow was there, but the song was in her heart.

Next to the Bible, I consider a hymn book of my own a most valuable worship aid. To prayerfully read the words of a great church hymn, such as Isaac Watts' "When I survey the wondrous cross," is a devotional experience. Memorizing the words and singing them throughout the week can be a spiritual blessing to any child of God, even if others might not consider the results grand opera.

In congregational singing we often pay more attention to the music than the words. Reading the stanzas as a poem at home helps us consider the meaning of the words. We learn that others have met the same trials we have, yet they sing God's praises.

Pastor Benson had a powerful voice. How I loved to hear him sing "How firm a foundation ye saints of the Lord." The congregation tried to follow him as he closed the hymnal for the last lines. Silver-haired, he raised his eyes, while the words rang out slower and slower, with emphasis: "I'll never, — no never, — *no never forsake.*" I found my faith strengthened.

Even if voices crack or flat, if vocal chords

are loose and give forth raspy sounds, singing aloud can brighten the day. Luther said it doesn't matter what singing apparatus we have, we should "Sing with the beak we have!"

Fanny Crosby, blind from birth, gave the church over 6000 hymns. Most of us have sung "Blessed assurance," "All the way my Savior leads me," and "To God be the glory, great things he hath done." Although Fanny Crosby wrote the last one over a century ago, it is popular today and is included in many hymnals.

Still time to sing? Yes, whether musically, off-key, or with spoken words, we can lift a hymn of praise to God.

Speaking to yourselves in psalms and hymns and spiritual songs, singing and making melody in your heart to the Lord. Eph. 5:19 KJ

O God, teach us to sing your praises for the great things you have done. Alleluia.

MARCHING ORDERS

One Sunday morning, confined by a sore throat to my home, I flipped on the TV and watched four consecutive religious programs. What color, music, beautiful young people, good sermons, and prayers! How good God is to remember those who are shut in.

There are, though, more dismal ways of being shut in than a temporary bout with a sore throat. Those totally deaf or blind, paralyzed or bedridden for months and years, have much to endure. No wonder the cry sometimes escapes, "God, let me die. I'm old and useless."

To many persons not hearing, seeing, or moving is a hopeless handicap. They are indeed real problems, but so long as we tackle real problems instead of brooding over or longing for the past, we are living in the present. God can use us. He has marching orders for us.

E. Stanley Jones in his book *The Divine Yes*, written after he suffered a serious stroke, relates that he was basking in the long life God had given him, with gratitude for his goodness, when suddenly he was stricken.

Through long nights and days he told himself that God still cared, that his faith was in Jesus Christ who would never let him down. The man recovered enough to write the book, his 29th.

If you are deaf or have to strain to catch every word, your special work may be different from that of those who hear well. If you can't see, God will hand you a job where eyes aren't important. If you can't move, or if you suffer pain, hang on. God is very close. He has marching orders for you!

Your special duty may we wrapped up in little things, consideration for those who care for you. If you can't make it on your own, God may commission you to show understanding and love to all who enter your room.

A college dean of women, who suffered six operations to destroy cancer, found God had marching orders for her in a hospital.

"In spite of the dark valley of pain and death," she says, "during one hospital stay God granted me the greatest privilege any of us can have—that of leading someone to the Savior.

"I would not have chosen the place or just those circumstances. He chose for me."

Zacchaeus accepted his handicap of being short. He climbed a sycamore tree and peered out of the green leaves to see what was going on. Then he heard the Master's voice, "Zacchaeus, come down. Today I'm coming to your house."

None of us is useless in God's sight. He needs all kinds of people to serve him. He needs old and young, those who go to work and meet people, those who stay home with leisure time, or are confined to bed. Those who see with their eyes and those who "see" with their hands. Those who hear with ears and those who "hear" with the heart. God has work for each of us as long as we live.

For I the Lord thy God will hold thy right hand, saying unto thee, Fear not; I will help thee. Isa. 41:13 KJ

Dear Father, thank you that we have awakened to another day. What do you have for us to do?

STUMBLING BLOCKS OR STEPPING-STONES

Are you shut in to isolated, inactive days? Shut in by four walls? It may be temporary, a broken leg or hip or surgery, but you're housebound.

One man declares, "Being housebound makes you feel that life is strewn with stumbling blocks, and not a stepping-stone in sight."

It's a situation where we easily panic and ask God for a blessing. By a blessing we mean, "Get me out, Lord."

And all the while the very shut-in experience may be a stepping-stone to a wider field of usefulness, one beyond our imagination.

Jesus told Peter that Satan wanted to test him. "But," Jesus added, "I have prayed for you that your faith fail not" (Luke 22:32). Not that Peter escape the testing, but that his faith fail not.

"Not me, Lord," Peter said. "I'm ready to go with you to jail or death." He stumbled

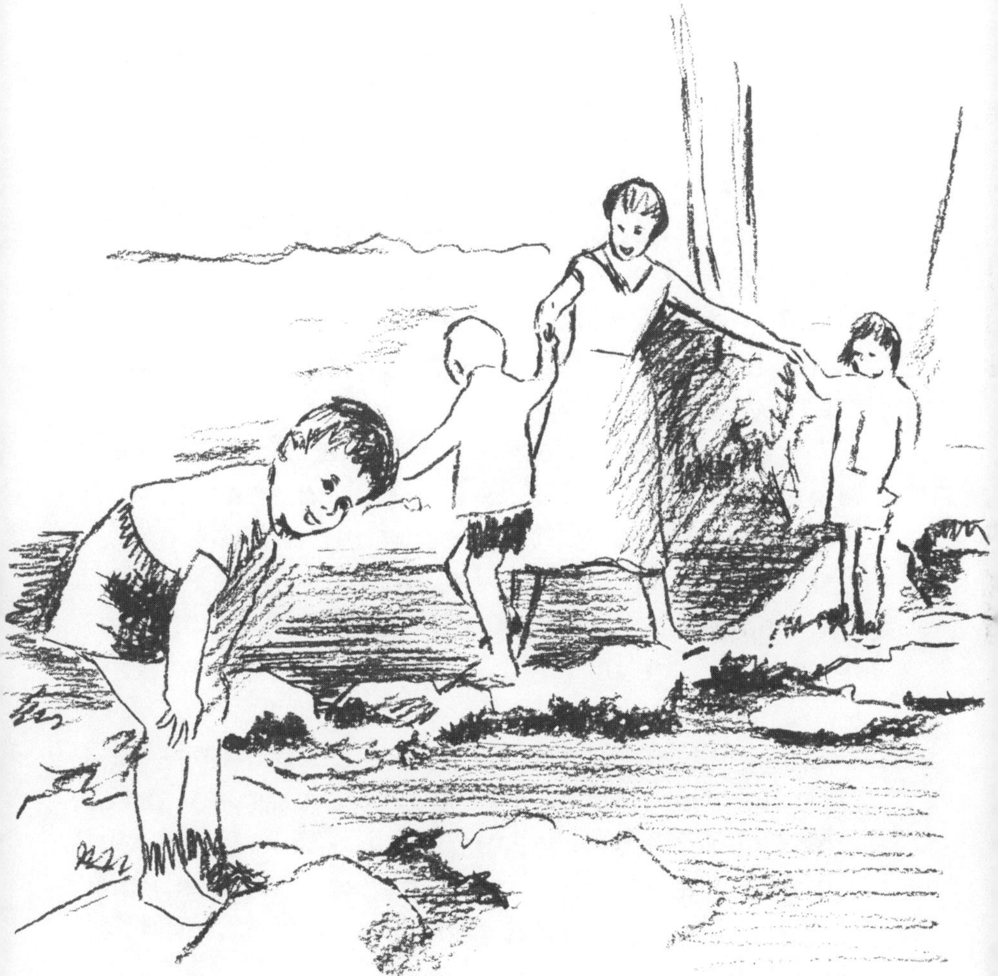

badly on that one. Just as Jesus predicted, Peter denied him three times. Although Peter didn't know it, the testing was a stepping-stone to great responsibility.

Shut in by four walls? It's time to rest in the Lord and look for stepping-stones. A quotation from Andrew Murray has been on my desk for years. The words are to this effect:

Whenever we are sorely tried, remember:
1. It is by God's will.
2. He will supply the grace needed.
3. He will make the trial a blessing.
4. He will deliver us at the right time.

With such an attitude stumbling blocks turn into stepping-stones.

"I thank God for my memory," a housebound woman said. "As I lie in bed or sit in my wheelchair I recall the good times of the past. The sunsets, forest trails. What I have seen I can see forever." She added, "I think of the miracle of the birth of my children without reliving any of the pain."

I knew what she meant, for I sometimes remember the summer picnics we used to have when my children were young. I relive the joy without the work of making sandwiches and potato salad. I forget the mosquitoes and the sunburn.

Our memories can be stepping-stones to joy.

Shut-in days can be used to enjoy armchair travel. Emily Dickinson wrote that she never saw a moor, but she knew what heather looked like. She never saw the sea, but she knew what a wave was like.

God has given us the gift of imagination. We can send for travel leaflets of far countries. We can read about the country in encyclopedia and library books. A friend has several years' issues of *The National Geographic*. Should she be housebound, she will take armchair journeys.

Socrates, that dispenser of wisdom, said, "Remember, no human condition is ever permanent, then you will not be overjoyed in good fortune nor too sorrowful in misfortune."

Rest in the Lord, and wait patiently for him.
Psalm 37:7 KJ

O Father, what a world you have given us to enjoy. Shut-in days give us the sense of stumbling blocks. Help us open the window and look out. Help us use our memory and imagination to discover the stepping-stones you have set before us.

GOD'S KNOCKING TIME

From counting sheep to relaxing muscles, from warm milk to sleeping pills, enough remedies for sleeplessness are around to tell us that the affliction is widespread.

When someone says, "I didn't sleep a wink last night," I can sympathize, for I have had similar nights. Usually I have no trouble sleeping, but once in a while there I am, either wide awake and fretting or half awake and fretting. I think the second state is worse.

If we're wide awake, we can turn on the light and read or write a letter, clean out the desk drawer, or make a snack. Being wide awake is a good time for intensive prayer. Sometimes I've wakened out of a sound sleep with someone's name in mind. I take that as God's "knocking time," a nudge that God wants me to pray.

But half awake and restless means we can't concentrate.

Some are in a keyed-up state because they

take to bed with them the day's unfinished business. The advice of those I've talked to is: never take problems to bed with you. Pray about them. Ask for forgiveness. Then hand the bundle over to God and block it out of mind. Tomorrow morning you may have to start on the knot where you left off, but for now, God is in charge while you sleep. He will not slumber.

Reading a light book, one that doesn't require deep thought, makes some people drowsy.

A woman who often has difficulty falling asleep says, "Pick a happy memory and relive it from beginning to end."

Another, now in her late 80s says, "When I can't sleep at night, I turn on the radio to the station that plays favorite hymns and sing right along with the music."

Others, who must be quiet in their homes, recall the words of hymns, poetry, or Scripture. Put Scripture verses on cards and memorize a verse or two every evening before sleep. You're too old to memorize? Retired Salvation Army Major John Jay Shearer, who recently celebrated his 104th birthday, says he spends time praying and memorizing Scripture every day.

Reading several psalms helps some I know.

A book of printed prayers can be helpful. The classic is John Baillie's *A Diary of Private Prayer.*

Thank God for the blessings of the past day. Name them one by one.

For those who still have trouble sleeping at night, John Oxenham has these words:

> Thank God for sleep!
> And when you cannot sleep,
> Still thank him that you live
> To lie awake.

When thou liest down, thou shalt not be afraid: yea, thou shalt lie down, and thy sleep shall be sweet. Proverbs 3:24 KJ

Heavenly Father, your Word tells us that you never sleep. Take charge of our doubts, fears, troubles while we sleep.

DON'T DESERT ME NOW

God had a reservation in a lions' den for Daniel that night. The Bible tells us Daniel had a right spirit, that he faithfully prayed to God. Yet God sent him to spend the night with lions kept for the purpose of tearing men apart and crunching their bones.

From reading about Daniel's life, I can't find that he reproached God for the calamity. There's no record he questioned God's wisdom. But I imagine he cried, "Lord, don't desert me now! You alone are my hope" (Jer. 17:17 LB). Perhaps he also said, "Thank you, Lord."

God's Word tells us to give thanks for all things. Giving thanks can open the floodgates of God's power and show he is able to deliver us.

Writing in *Upper Room Disciplines*, Jo Kimmel declares that the most powerful of all prayers may be "Thank you, Lord." She tells of being in severe pain from a fall. She couldn't stand, sit, or lie down without excruciating pain. Remembering that she was to give thanks in all circumstances, even though she didn't feel thankful, she prayed aloud, "Thank you, Lord." Within 10 minutes the pain let up and after that night never returned.

Not that we rejoice *in* adversity, but rather that we see it as one of those "all things" that work for good. God wants his people to have "the garment of praise for the spirit of heaviness" (Isa. 61:3).

Thank you, Lord. Not for the death of a loved partner, or the disabilities of age, not for insufficient income, nor conflict with relatives. But thank you for what you will do for us and others through our adversity, even though, as with Daniel, the explanation is hidden from us.

My apartment door has a peephole so that when someone knocks, I can look out and see who's there. The view of the hall is limited. I can't see the stairway the caller climbed, nor the other apartment doors. All I see is the one knocking.

When God allows adversity to knock on our door, all we see is what is right in front of us. Usually we don't like what we see, so we rebel, and resentment surfaces. All because we don't have God's wide-angle viewpoint of the past, the present, the future.

Instead, as William Law suggests, "Whatever seeming calamity happens to you, if you thank and praise God for it, you turn it into a blessing."

Thanking God for all things brings us his power to live through our "den of lions." Instead of heaviness of heart, we discover with joy that our God is able to deliver us. Whether the calamity is removed or remains, he never deserts us.

I will sing of thy power; . . . for thou hast been my defence and refuge in the day of my trouble. Psalm 59:16 KJ

Dear Father in heaven, whatever you choose to do to us or through us, we will give you the praise.

SOJOURNERS

"I don't believe in life after death," said a woman near me at a luncheon.

A devout Christian across the table stammered. "How—how can you say that? What church do you go to? Don't you read the Bible?"

"There's no use trying to change me," the first one said with a pleasant smile.

"How can you face each day?" the other continued. "If I didn't know I'd see my Savior and loved ones, I would despair."

"I don't believe in life after death," the woman repeated.

Those who have no faith may refuse to believe in the afterlife. But Christians believe God's Word that we are sojourners, temporary residents, of this world. Still we have questions. Death is a mystery and many are curious about the hereafter.

"If a man die, shall he live again?" cried Job in his soul struggle.

Will we see the Savior after death?

Will we see and know our loved ones?

It is said that when Sir Walter Scott faced death, he cried, "Bring me the Book."

"What book?" they asked.

"There is only one Book—the Bible."

In that book we read how Jesus gave his disciples hope. "Because I live, you shall live also" (John 14:19).

Fanny Crosby enlarges on the theme in her song "Face to face with Christ my Savior." Songwriter Campbell declares with haunting melody in "The next step" that "The next hand you shake might be the hand of the Savior."

We who are children of God through spiritual birth have confidence that to be absent from the body means to be present with the Lord (2 Cor. 5:8) in the place he has prepared for us.

After our mother died, my brother wrote a detailed letter. "Mother went home to be with the Lord early this morning." When I showed the letter to a friend, she looked puzzled. "What does he mean, 'went home'?"

The book of Hebrews gives assurance for such hope. After naming many Bible notables famous for their faith, the writer says, "These all died in faith . . . and confessed that they were strangers and pilgrims on the earth" (Heb. 11:13 KJ).

Will we know our loved ones? David fasted and prayed when his little son lay dying. When the child died, David rose up, took food, and worshipped God. At once the busybodies criticized David. He defended himself. "Now the child is dead, why should I fast? Can I bring him back?"

Then he spoke words that have comforted others through the ages. "I shall go to him, but he shall not return to me" (2 Sam. 12:23 KJ).

While not fully understanding the mystery of death, we have faith in the Lord Jesus and the promises in the Word of God. Along with Emerson we can say, "All I have seen teaches me to trust the Creator for all I have not seen."

I am the resurrection and the life; he who believes in me, though he die, yet shall he live.
John 11:25

Dear Lord Jesus, we can't imagine what the place is like you have prepared for us in the Father's house. We love you and believe nothing can separate us from the love of God.

BLESSED ASSURANCE

"I don't want to talk about death," a woman in her 70s said. "I'm afraid to die." Is there a reason for her fear?

No one disputes the statistic that one out of one dies. Death comes to everyone, culling heads of state and men behind bars, releasing the aged from pain and cutting off children from carefree activity.

How many times have we wept after losing a friend or dear one. "He's lived a good long life," someone says, as though that settles it. One more death.

It's not just a statistic, though, when it's *my* death we're talking about, or yours. When it's time for us to merge into that highway toward death where there's never a "no vacancy" sign, that's what is inevitable. That's what we have to accept. The end of my face which I see in the mirror—my legs, my arms, my breathing. The end of the life I prize after 60 or 70 years or more of living. It's my death I need to accept.

And how do we do that?

One of the windfall benefits of old age is there's more time to enjoy each new day—the sun, flowers, and trees. We forget about being selfish and critical of others when we are delighting in the love of God's Son. Now there's time to tidy up a bit, to get ready for that final journey.

We're not in a hurry, but we want to learn all we can about what lies ahead. We're like the boy who asked, "What does it mean to die? I don't want to do it. I just want to know." Or like the Apostle Paul who had a desire to depart and be with Christ. Still he felt he had work to do; he wasn't quite ready (Phil. 1:23-24).

One time I visited a friend in the hospital who said, "I'm not afraid of death. I'm trusting in God's promise of eternal life." Still her face showed apprehension. "It's the *dying* I'm afraid of. Long-drawn-out illness, pain, helplessness, money running out. Alone...."

It's true no human can go all the way through the Valley of the Shadow with us—not husband, wife, child, doctor, or nurse. What a lonely experience, except for one thing. Jesus said, "I will send you another Comforter." The literal meaning of *comforter* is "one called alongside to help." And that Comforter, the Holy Spirit, who lives within the believer, will conduct us safely through dying into God's presence.

In a country cemetery a headstone without a name marks one grave. On the stone is carved the word *Forgiven*. Nothing else.

Ah! The assurance of forgiveness.

In whom we have redemption through his blood, the forgiveness of sins, according to the riches of his grace. Eph. 1:7 KJ

Keep us aware of your presence, Lord, even when we do not have strength or wit to pray.

CUTTING OUT CLUTTER

Over a period of six years we moved from a large eight-room house to a small six-room house to a four-room apartment. Each move entailed giving and throwing away, or selling, furniture, dishes, tools, letters, and papers.

So it was with surprise I heard my daughter say, "Mom, you like the cluttered look."

Afterwards I sat down and tried to see my rooms objectively. I looked at my collection of handbells. I once heard a man declare that when we have more than six of one item, we have a collection. I had collections of teapots, trivets, Bibles, picture albums and books.

Then I saw all the dear items my grandchildren had made me in kindergarten and at camp. I peered into the storage closet, opened drawers and chests, and poked into boxes.

Why was I clutching all those items? Sentiment? Habit? Future need? The thought nagged me that I might be holding onto articles I never looked at that someone else could use. Would my family value what I leave behind, I wondered. How can we make it easier for our families to dispose of our belongings when the time comes?

I remember two young women who, after their mother's death, spent nearly two weeks sorting out her possessions. From attic to basement the house was packed with the accumulation of 40 years of living in one house. The daughters didn't know the value of some items. They spent time on worthless bundles of correspondence. Before the house was finally cleared and sold, hard feelings developed with other relatives and friends.

Can the answer be to declutch now? I typed instructions on a card and propped it where I could see it.

How to declutch:
Give away or throw away one item every day.

At first I gave and threw away by 4s and 5s, sending boxes to the Salvation Army, the Goodwill, and a children's orphanage.

I have a friend who is making the job easier for her heirs. She writes on masking tape the name of the one she wants to have her various possessions. Then she puts the tape on the bottom of the article.

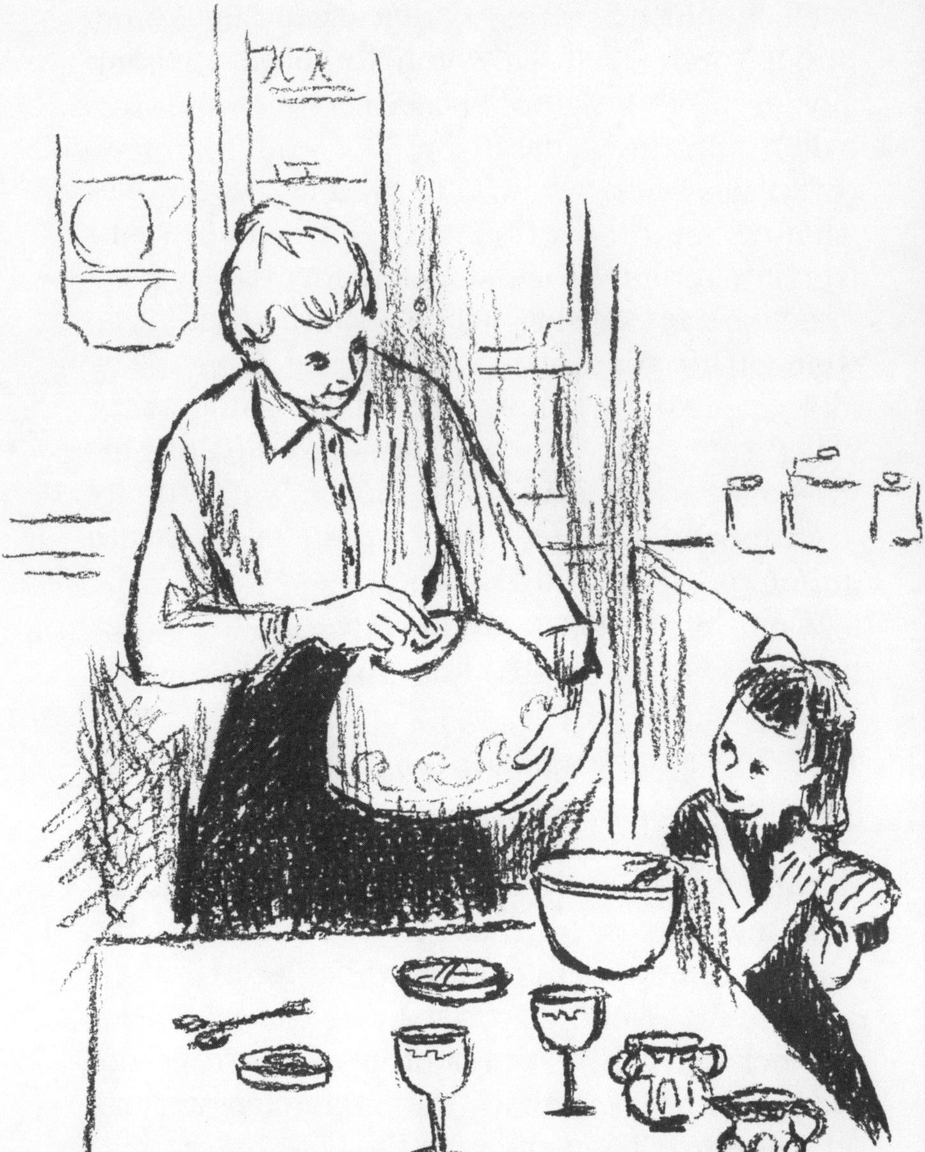

On her 80th birthday my grandmother found herself with 31 descendents and cupboards of silver, china, and valuable curios accumulated over a lifetime. As Christmas and birthday gifts, she gave one of her fine possessions to each of her family. Not only did we gain the treasures, but she enjoyed our happiness.

Other widows have told me that each season they check their clothes closet. If a garment has not been worn three or four times, they weed it out, sending it to someone in need or where it will be used.

It's true we older ones often have one thing going for us that younger people don't. We lose our bent for acquiring things. But somehow we tighten our hold on the possessions we already have.

All these things we have. Could someone else use them?

Lay not up for yourselves treasures upon earth. Matt. 6:19 KJ

Father, we have used and enjoyed our possessions for a long time. Show us how we can relinquish some items and give pleasure to other people.

SILVER, GOLD, AND CATTLE

"The biggest problem facing the aging," an authority on gerontology says, "is not that they are frequently ill, but that they are usually broke."

I remember a time in my childhood when our family was "broke." We didn't trust the government for food stamps and Social Security, and there were times when we didn't know what we would eat the next day. More than once we were certain God directed a kind neighbor to supply our need.

Today financial insecurity engulfs hundreds of thousands of older people. I once heard a minister say that security in old age rests not on money, but on what we can do without.

Or it may rest in simple trust that everything belongs to God, the silver and the gold, the cattle on a thousand hills, and that he knows our needs.

With such faith we can be content, knowing that God entrusts more money to some, less to others. Whatever the amount, the way we spend our money indicates our values.

I'm glad that as a young person in our church I learned the principle of stewardship and tithing, or proportionate giving. (Those who tithe usually give a tenth of their income to the church as a bare minimum and often give more.)

I learned about tithing, too, from one dear woman of my childhood, a faithful steward of what God gave her. Very little money came into her hands. Still she gave a tenth of whatever she had to the minister, those in need, and others. Our family enjoyed packages of cleaned fish caught by her husband, loaves of bread, and jars of luscious pears and peaches from her kitchen. When she couldn't give food, she gave flowers from her garden.

One day the minister handed her a copy of a poem titled "Others." "Reminds me of you," he said.

The experience of one couple is an example of stewardship. They carefully figured the income they would have after they stopped working. Then for two years they lived on that amount, banking the remainder. "It wasn't easy," the wife says. "But we proved we could retire on schedule."

Five years later the man says, "Because of inflation we have had to cut corners in order to give to God's work. I had thought insufficient income was something that happened to the old folks across the street, not us."

No two ways about it, if income is insufficient, we have to get more, spend less or do without. Recently a widow told me, "When I saw what my income would be, I moved to a small town where I can walk every place, and it's easier to do without things."

Bill Gothard, director of Basic Youth Conflicts Seminar, sets forth the idea that if we put God first, he makes our income stretch by eliminating emergency expenses that eat up money.

The earth is the Lord's and the fulness thereof; the world and they that dwell therein.

Ps. 24:1 KJ

O God, implant in our hearts the faith to trust your goodness even for the necessities of life.

ONLY ONE VOTE

"Nobody Votes in My Town" was the title of an article in a national newspaper. The article explained that it was not because the inhabitants didn't want to vote. Convicted of serious crime, they had lost the right to vote. The town referred to was the state penitentiary.

As American citizens we have the right to vote. But what happens? After the campaigning and mud-slinging and expense, the winner in the 1968 Presidential election won by a narrow margin. Nearly half the voters wanted the other candidate. Citizens who failed to vote outnumbered either of the two sides who did vote.

The United States Bureau of the Census reports that in the November 1974 election 141 million Americans were eligible to vote. Only 62 percent registered and only 45 percent voted.

A common excuse is, "What's the use? I'm only one person." But voters can alter laws, change conditions, put men into office, and drive them out.

Dwight Eisenhower once said that we are not discharging our responsibilities as American citizens unless we are concerned about our government and do something about it. "You do that job," he said, "by voting and getting others to vote in every election."

We may also not be discharging our Christian responsibilities by failing to vote. One of the two commandments Jesus gave us is to love our neighbor. Voting on issues that concern people is one way we show our love for our neighbor. We can work toward better health, welfare, education, and safety for all. We can help victims of injustice.

Are there unfair laws? We can learn facts, read articles, listen to news reports. We can talk to those concerned, write our congressmen. We can work toward change.

U.S. Senator Mark Hatfield declared, "Government at all levels is no better than the demands of the citizens."

Dr. Ethel Percy Andrus, founder of the American Association of Retired Persons, once said, "We who are older are free to have the conviction, the right, to keep on being in the stream of life."

I like the way a grandmother puts it in a letter to an editor. "We aren't through yet. We pay taxes and we will be governed by the crop of kids coming up. We belong in PTA and at open school-board meetings."

Voting is the power to influence government, to show our concern for others. With time now to study needs and issues, every aging person has an obligation to vote.

In any election all we get is one vote.

I urge that petitions, prayers, intercessions, and thanksgivings be offered for all men; for sovereigns and all in high office, that we may lead a tranquil and quiet life in full observance of religion and high standards of morality.

1 Tim. 2:1-2 NEB

Father, make us aware of the value of our one vote.

TAKE PEN IN HAND

A well-organized person I sometimes meet walked into the stationery store with me the other day.

"I need more carbon paper," she said.

"What are you writing?" I asked.

"Letters mostly. I make carbon copies and paste them in a scrapbook, together with the letters I'm answering. My journal."

"Like Samuel Pepys and George Washington?" I asked.

She laughed. "No editor will snatch my diary. But I forget so easily. I keep copies of my letters so I won't repeat myself, and also to have a record of important events in my life."

Not many of us keep journals or diaries or even notebooks today. Are we therefore losing valuable history our families may be interested in later? Older people find the discipline of writing down thoughts, beliefs, hopes, doubts, and experiences adds an extra dimension to life.

The noble ladies of the fifteenth century left the world a diary, a record that is world famous. They spent their days embroidering what is known as the Bayeaux tapestry. Detailed pictures tell the story of the Norman Conquest. The tapestry is 230 feet long and 20 inches wide, with hundreds of inscriptions in Latin and pictures of men and ships in action, all embroidered in colored wool.

Not always valued as it is now, the tapestry covered wagons during the French Revolution. Later it was rescued and is now carefully preserved in Bayeaux, France, in a special building, protected by glass cases.

A notebook can be a fine place to jot down beliefs and ideas about God and people. I like the advice Florida Scott Maxwell gives in her book *The Measure of My Days*. "If a grandmother wants to put her foot down, the only safe place to do it these days is in a notebook."

Writing letters can sometimes keep us out of trouble. A woman who had had unpleasant words with her sister couldn't sleep that night for thinking about the squabble. She got up and wrote a two-page letter.

"I got everything off my chest," she told me. Humbly she added, "Then I tore up the letter."

The next morning she called her sister with happy results.

My father wrote monthly letters to each of his four children, which constitute a sort of diary of his later years. In his 80s he researched, compiled and wrote a 120-page history of his family, presenting bound copies to his descendants.

Members of a Bible study group who wrote down what the Savior meant to them learned that the act of putting their faith into words strengthened them.

Letter, diary, history, testimony—all can be worthwhile writing to leave for future generations.

The grace of our Lord Jesus Christ be with you. 1 Thess. 5:28

Dear Lord, the letters in your Book, though written so long ago, are fresh and bright today. May we describe your love and goodness as we write.

FOOTWASHERS

I saw another footwasher the other day. That makes half a dozen in the last two weeks. To be sure, none of them produced an actual basin with Lifebuoy soap and a towel. And nobody took off shoes and stockings.

It's easy, though, to catch the similarity of the footwashing I mean and the demonstration by Jesus in the upper room.

In Bible days a servant washed the dusty feet of those who came for supper. But at the Lord's Supper no servant performed the task. Instead, Jesus laid aside his robe, picked up a towel, poured water into a basin, and knelt before each disciple in turn, washing his feet.

Then Jesus said, "If I then, your Lord and Master, have washed your feet, ye also ought to wash one another's feet" (John 13:14 KJ).

"Footwashing," said a man who practices the literal act, "is undertaken by humble folk when they lay aside their garments of pride, kneel, and wash the feet of another."

Jesus knew we needed the humbling experience of footwashing, literal or symbolic.

When the custodian of one small church said he would like to visit his native Sweden for 10 weeks, the church board of trustees agreed to clean the church in his absence.

Each Friday night during the sweltering summer found some perspiring board member and his wife hard at work. The pastor, a department store executive, a buyer for a chain store, a commercial artist, and others took turns.

A $3-an-hour supermarket cashier sent her $1000 vacation savings to a Vietnamese who was trying to get his wife and two sons out of Vietnam.

"He needs money to cut through red tape," she said.

Another footwasher, though he wouldn't call it that, is Hugh McLeod. A former executive for a national company, he took an early retirement to accept a dollar-a-year job as assistant to the president of Bethel College, St. Paul, Minnesota.

When asked why he would devote so much time to a job without pay, Hugh said, "I can't think of a better way to keep busy in retirement and serve the Lord."

Then there was the time when we walked into our church foyer for the children's Christmas program. Ahead of us one little girl unswallowed her supper. Consternation took over.

"Debby, why didn't you. . . . " "What will we do?" "Watch out!"

While others cringed, the pastor ran downstairs, came back with a mop and pail, and righted things in a jiffy.

Another "footwasher" is the black man who calls at a nursing home once a week to clip finger and toe nails of those who can't.

Footwashers are alert to servant jobs. They understand what S. S. Kresge meant. "Find out where you can render a service and then render it. The rest is up to the Lord."

Whoever will be chief among you, let him be your servant. Matt. 20:27 KJ

O Savior, it is easy to do what serves and pleases us. Thank you for your example of footwashing. Help us to know the joy that comes with serving others for your sake.

THE TIME
OF YOUR LIFE

Where you live you may be able to look out your window and lift your eyes to the everlasting hills. You can watch the four seasons transforming fertile fields.

Or you can walk along the seashore, hearing the unending waves crash against rocks.

You may know the peacefulness of strolling down a tree-arched street, with a loved dog on leash, or fishing on a quiet lake, or watching the birds at the backyard feeder.

Wherever we live, the first picture our window frames when we rise in the morning is a patch of God's sky.

And whether we see the pale pink of apple blossoms in that picture, the green of tall corn growing, or a high rise outlined against the dawn, the heavens declare the glory of God. The precision and order of the world make us fall on our knees and worship God the Creator.

How good God is to give us senses to enjoy his world—the warm breezes of May or the blizzards of January. And if eyes or ears have failed, we can remember such pictures.

Older people who have gotten out of their rocking chairs (if not literally, then figuratively) are the ones who are having the time of their lives. Not for them is that everything-is-over feeling. They've made an inventory of their blessings with the joyful results that they are rich. They keep working long past retirement age. Or they travel, struggle with new activities, adjust to new ideas, and change.

Roy L. Smith once wrote, "That situation which compels us to think, exert every effort, and to invest our supreme powers is a blessing, even though it be disguised as a hardship."

Those who are less energetic or confined to home can sew a dress, knit afghans, build a doll's house for the pure joy of making something. For 10 years after she reached 85 the mother of one of my friends set herself the goal of learning one new handwork pattern each year. She wanted to make gifts for her numerous descendants.

Many not so active older ones are examples to those younger, as I learned at an evening prayer circle when a young woman prayed:

"Dear God, thank you for the old people in

our church. I see their beautiful contented faces, full of wisdom and experience and patience and faith in Jesus Christ. I want to know these older Christians better. I want to grow like them. Amen."

Laughter is also important, for the more we find to laugh about the better company we will be. "A good laugh is sunshine in a house," said William Thackeray. I laughed when I read these words of columnist Hal Boyle: "The way to tell whether you are old is if Uncle Sam sends you more money than you send him."

"Laughter tells us that it is a crazy, ridiculous, preposterous world, and that we had better learn to laugh or we shall find it impossible to live in it," writes Sherwood Wirt.

God has allowed us to live to the present time. The last third of a long life can be the best years if we *live* them.

March on, my soul, with strength!
Judges 5:21 LB

Father, our times are in your hands. Help us to accept old age as your gift, knowing we shall not pass this way again. Give us expectations and your power to make them happen.

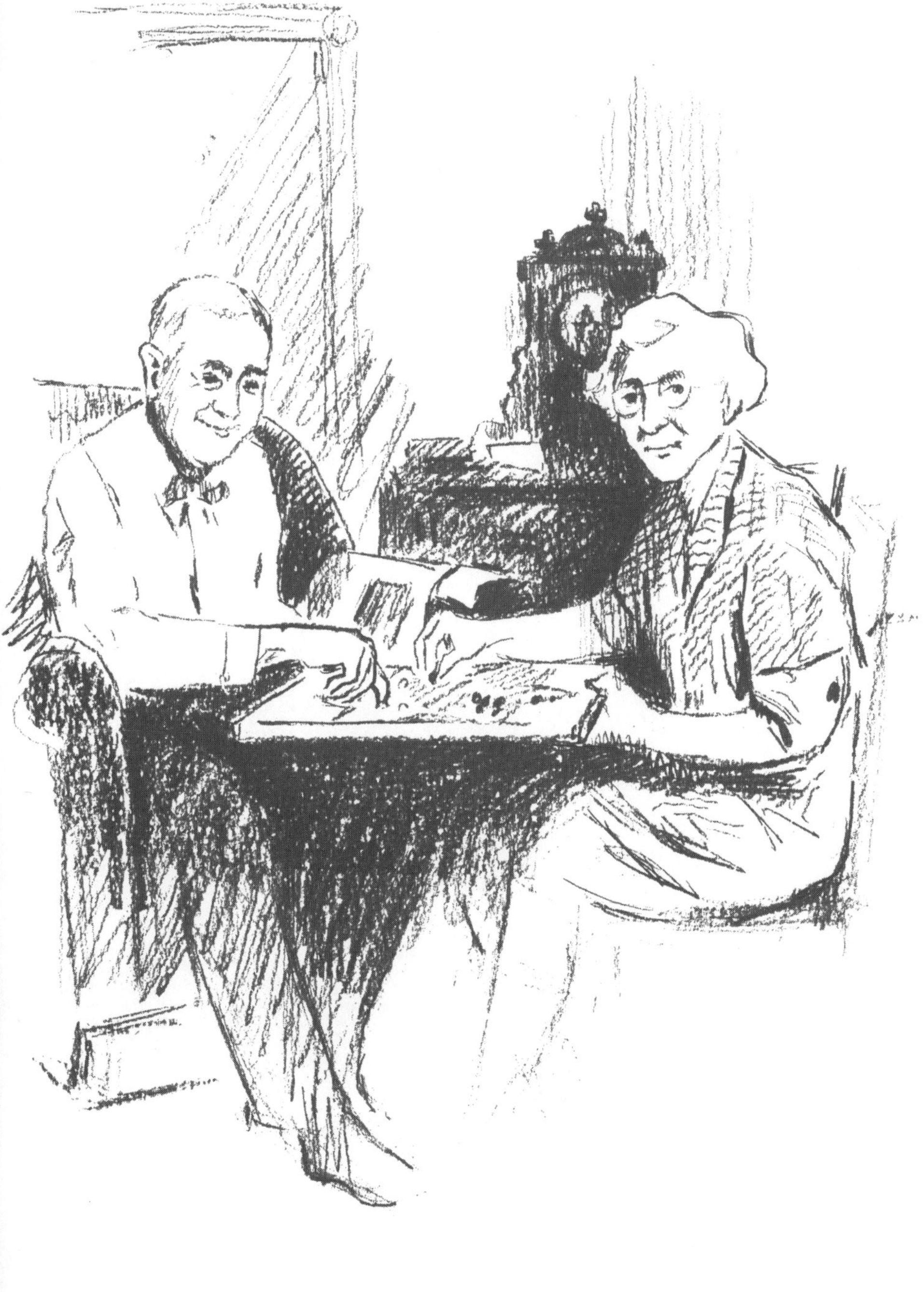